D0591135

STRAWBERRIES

&

CHEAM

Also by Harry Secombe and published by Robson Books

FICTION
Twice Brightly
Welsh Fargo

NON-FICTION
Goon Abroad
The Harry Secombe Diet Book
Harry Secombe's Highway
The Highway Companion

FOR CHILDREN
Katy and the Nurgla
The Nurgla's Magic Tear

STRAWBERRIES

&

CHEAM

The Autobiography

of

HARRY SECOMBE

Vol 2
1951–1996

Robson Books

First published in Great Britain in 1996 by Robson Books
Ltd, Bolsover House, 5– 6 Clipstone Street, London W1P 8LE

Copyright © 1996 Sir Harry Secombe

The right of Sir Harry Secombe to be identified as author of
this work has been asserted by him in accordance with the
Copyright, Designs and Patents Act 1988

British Library Cataloguing in Publication Data
A catalogue record for this title is available from the British
Library

ISBN 1 86105 048 8

Photoset in North Wales by Derek Doyle & Associates, Mold,
Flintshire. Printed in Great Britain by Butler & Tanner Ltd,
London and Frome.

To Myra
who has always been there for me.

.

Why *Strawberries and Cheam* for a title, I hear you ask. Well, I called the first volume of my autobiography *Arias and Raspberries* because it encapsulated my career as a performer, and for this one I wanted something to sum up my private life. For over thirty years my family and I lived in Cheam. The strawberries? We grew them in the garden. I hope that answers your question.

Now read on . . .

Contents

Acknowledgements

Just as there is no such thing as a one man show, no book is the work of the author alone. I owe a great debt to my elder daughter, Jennifer, who has had to sort out my scribbled notes from various exercise books and put them in some semblance of order, to my younger daughter, Katy, who did a lot of research on the films and theatre productions I have been involved in, and to David, my younger son, for helping to transcribe some of my manuscript.

My thanks go to my editor, Louise Dixon, who has had the unenviable task of ploughing through the morass of paper and making sense of it all.

Thanks also to Ronnie Cass for his help with the *Highway* chapter, to the Theatre Museum, Covent Garden and to the British Film Institute.

Preface

It seemed as if the elements had conspired to bid Peter Sellers a final, dramatic farewell. Thunder rolled around the black sky, lightning flickered overhead and rain lashed down as we drove into the crematorium.

In spite of the weather there were crowds of people outside the chapel.

'Look at them,' said Michael Bentine, who had been unusually serious on the journey up from the house. He and his wife, Clementina, had decided to come to the funeral with Myra and me.

'We'd better make a dash for it.' I eyed the torrential rain as I spoke.

Mike was the first out, followed by Clementina and Myra, and I was a poor fourth, hampered by my girth from leaping with any sort of agility from the front passenger seat of the Rolls.

Inside the chapel, a small group had already assembled in the vestry. Tony Snowdon greeted Myra with a warm kiss and David Lodge and Graham Stark came across to join us. We were all smiling nervously, making bright conversation, still too shocked by Peter's death to know what to say to each other. Spike Milligan had not yet turned up and there was speculation as to whether Peter's second wife, Britt Ekland, would make an appearance. Theo Cowan, an old friend and Peter's publicist, introduced the weeping widow, Lynne Sellers, and Denis Selinger, who had been our old mate's agent for many years, smiled and nodded in our direction. He looked lost without his pipe.

Father John Hester, to whom Peter had turned so many times for guidance in the past and who was an ardent *Goon Show* fan, announced that it was time for the service to begin.

We filed into the chapel and took our seats. My eyes turned to the coffin, unable to take in the fact that it contained the body of an old friend. Henry Crun and Bloodknock and Gritpype Thynne and Clouseau were in there. And poor old Bluebottle had been 'deaded' for the last time.

Only a few days earlier we had planned to meet for dinner – just the three of us – Spike, Peter and myself.

'It's about time we had a meal together before either one of us finds himself walking behind a coffin saying "We should have had a meal together".' That's what Peter had said to Spike on the phone from Gstaad.

So Spike had called me to fix a date and we made it for the previous Tuesday, but Peter had collapsed that afternoon, a couple of hours before we were due to meet. He never really regained consciousness after that.

And now here we were. There was a stir in the chapel and Spike came in. Behind him was Britt Ekland.

The four Goons were together for the last time. Three greying, respectable gents come to say farewell to our dear friend. Where were the four frenetic lads of the 50s, the anti-establishment rebels of yesterday?

I shifted uneasily in my seat as John Hester spoke lightly

and well about Peter as a man and as an artist. In the pew across the aisle Spike was looking down into his folded hands. Alongside me Mike was nodding gravely in agreement at what was being said.

Then, his short address over, Father Hester announced that it was Peter's wish that a certain piece of music should be played at his funeral. In accordance with that wish, a recording would now be played.

We all sat back, dutifully solemn, waiting for the music to begin. I didn't know much about Peter's taste in serious music. I expected Sibelius, perhaps, or maybe an extract from Dvořák's New World Symphony.

There was a crackle on the loudspeakers and through the chapel came the sound of Glenn Miller's 'In the Mood', an old dance band foxtrot which was completely out of keeping with the occasion.

I looked along at Spike and he grinned back. On my left, Mike Bentine was stifling a giggle. Suddenly it was all as it should be. There were smiles all round again and I gave Myra's hand a reassuring squeeze. I let the music wash over me.

The Goons

We are old men now, we who were the angry young men of comedy – Spike, Mike and me, grizzled veterans cloaked in respectability; Commanders of the Order of the British Empire to a man; absorbed by the establishment; our teeth drawn and our illustrious partner Peter dead and buried, only to be resurrected in a flurry of tabloid controversy at least once a year.

Goon but not forgotten.

It is amazing to me how the *Goon Show* still lives on. Only last year the Goon Show Preservation Society held a three-day seminar at a Bournemouth hotel and fans came from all over the place – including America and Canada. The recordings that the BBC put out every year appear on the bestseller list every Christmas and, surprisingly, the royalties have increased over the last couple of years.

The show, then billed as *Those Crazy People*, was first broadcast on 28 May 1951. At that time the profession was full of stand-up comics who came on, told a string of jokes and finished either with a song or a dance. We were different. The Grafton Arms in Strutton Ground, Westminster, was our unofficial headquarters where the four of us would meet up and get high on drink and each other's company. We were all in the same boat then – young ex-servicemen determined to overthrow the established comedy of the day and create something which would appeal to the kind of people with whom we had served. We all thought that there was more to comedy than telling jokes about mothers-in-law and a funny thing happening to us on the way to the theatre. James Thomas of the *News Chronicle* said of the first series, 'Goon humour is obviously crazy and clever. It will either be loved or detested.'

Our backgrounds were very different. Spike was born in India, the son of an Irish RSM in the Indian Army.

When I first met him he was Lance-Sergeant Milligan, Terence A, and one of the crew of a large 7.2 gun howitzer which had been installed in a gun-pit insecurely dug in the hard rock of a Tunisian plateau. His howitzer was being fired by a lanyard – a rope attached to the firing lever which was used when the gun crew was not quite sure of what might happen. As the sergeant pulled the lanyard, the crew turned their backs to the gun as it fired, and when they turned round, the gun had disappeared.

At the time I was in an artillery regiment deployed nearby, and I was sitting in a small wireless truck at the foot of a sizeable cliff. Suddenly there was an enormous noise as some monstrous object fell from the sky quite close to us. There was considerable confusion, and in the middle of it all the flap of the truck was pulled open and a young helmeted Milligan asked, 'Anybody seen a gun?'

When I was demobbed in 1946, I started at the Windmill Theatre, where I had the good fortune to meet Michael Bentine. He was half of an act called Sherwood and Forest, and played the drums while Tony Sherwood played piano. I first saw him when he and his partner did the dress rehearsal for the show that followed the one I was in. From the beginning we found that we had the same sense of the ridiculous. We used to sit in the Lyons Corner House in Coventry Street and spend most of the night over a cup of coffee and beans on toast, sometimes pretending we were Russian ... until we picked on a Hungarian waiter who spoke Russian.

Although Mike's mother was English, his father was a distinguished Peruvian physicist and he refers to himself as the 'only Peruvian born on the Watford bypass'. Of the four of us, he was the most cerebral, having gone to Eton and the Lycée in Paris. At the beginning, he was also the only married man among us.

Peter Sellers was the only one of us who had a 'show business' background. His mother came from the Mendoza family, a well-known name in the theatre, and his father was a pit orchestra pianist. Peter was more professionally experienced than we were because he had played the drums in a band before the war. I was introduced to Peter at a radio broadcast I was doing for the Third Programme. The producer was Pat Dixon, a man with an ear for unusual comedy who was always on the look out for new talent. It was said that Peter had recently got himself a broadcast by the simple expedient of ringing Pat Dixon and, using the voice of another radio producer, recommending this new comic Peter Sellers to him. Minutes later, Sellers turned up at Dixon's office and was booked on the spot.

I was very impressed with Peter, by his friendliness and by the uncanny way he had of becoming the person he was impersonating. I was always amazed at the way he could shrink himself down for Bluebottle and then, seconds later, puff himself out for Bloodnock. Yet when he was called upon to do his own natural voice, he was always worried. 'I can't, lads,' he'd say. 'I don't know what I sound like.'

So it was that this motley quartet got together and started stirring the ingredients that went into the making of the

Goon Show. As I mentioned earlier, our unofficial headquarters was the Grafton Arms, run by the very gallant Major Jimmy Grafton, who, besides being a Westminster city councillor and a publican, was also a scriptwriter for Derek Roy, a regular comedian on the popular Sunday evening radio show *Variety Bandbox*. In due course, Jimmy became my agent. Our name for him was KOGVOS – 'Keeper of Goons and Voice of Sanity'.

Larry Stephens, an ex-commando who had served in Burma, worked with Spike on the early scripts and was another character who was tuned in to our wavelength.

For several years, Spike and Peter lived in a block of flats in Shepherd's Hill, north London, while I was living in Cheam, well south of the Thames. It was not unnatural then that being in such close proximity to each other sometimes led to the occasional spat between Spike and Peter. I would always know about it because I would get a phone call from the producer asking me to get along to rehearsals early on the Sunday morning to act as a kind of pacifier when the other two arrived. As far as I can remember, any differences they had would soon dissipate when the first read-through began.

As the second series wore on, Mike Bentine began to show signs that he was not too happy with the way things were going. When we all sat around discussing the show, he and Spike used to throw off ideas for scripts like sparks from a Catherine Wheel and it became inevitable that when some of these ideas actually appeared in the script, both would claim authorship. This led to some friction, and Dennis Main Wilson, the producer of the first three series, did not seem to be able to control us. After all, we were all about the same age and, like most ex-servicemen, we were not too willing to accept authority. We had had enough of that.

I was not privy to the other reasons why Mike decided to leave the *Goon Show*. My Variety commitments took me all over the country, and the only time I met the others was on the Sunday of the recording, so I was not aware of any power struggles that might have been going on.

Looking back on those days, I realize that I must have been surprisingly naïve. In any event, I was sorry to see Michael go. He went on to do great things on his own and was the first of us to make a name for himself.

On a typical *Goon Show* recording day, I would arrive at the Camden Theatre at around 2.30, musing on which car Peter had rolled up in. He was always changing his cars. As I entered the stage door I'd sing a burst of 'Return to Sorrento' in reply to which Sellers, lying in a prone position and playing the bongos, would cry 'It's Singo, the approaching tenor, folks,' and Milligan would announce my arrival with a NAAFI pianist's rendition of 'We'll Keep a Welcome' and a shout of 'Ah! The well-known danger to shipping has arrived. Ned of Wales is here!'

I'd reply with a raspberry and then the jokes would begin – mostly gags of a scatological nature.

Then it was time for our producer to try to exert some control over us (you could tell the producer by the worry lines on his forehead), and get us to have a look at the script. This was the time we all loved best. Peter and I would fall around giggling as we read the script for the first time. Spike would watch anxiously for our reactions to his efforts before joining in the general laughter.

Spike used to drive the studio managers mad with his insistence on getting the sound effects he wanted. In the beginning, when the programme was recorded on disc, it was extremely difficult to achieve the right sound effect. There were, I think, four turntables on the go simultaneously, with different sounds being played on each – chickens clucking, Big Ben striking, donkeys braying, massive explosions, ship's sirens – all happening at once.

It was only when tape came into use that Spike felt really

happy with the effects – although I do remember one particular time when he wanted to record the sound of someone being hit with a sockful of custard. He tried all sorts of ways to get the desired squelch, but to no avail. Eventually, he went into the Camden Theatre canteen and asked the very helpful Scottish lady behind the counter to make him an egg custard. 'Certainly, Spike,' she said, knowing that he sometimes ordered fancy meals on account of his weak stomach. 'Come back in twenty minutes.'

When he returned, the canteen lady proudly presented him with an earthenware bowl of egg custard, beautifully prepared with a sprinkling of nutmeg on the top.

'Here you are, Spike,' she said warmly. Spike thanked her and immediately began to take off the grey woollen army socks he often wore. She watched in utter amazement as he proceeded to spoon the contents of the bowl into both socks. She gave a little whimper and ran into the kitchen.

Back in the studio, Spike had already placed a sheet of three-ply wood near to a microphone. Swinging one of his socks around his head, he hurled it against the wood. The result wasn't quite what he wanted, so he did the same with the other sock. Alas, that too failed to produce the elusive SPLAT he was looking for. Realizing that he only had two feet and that nobody else would volunteer to try again, he stomped off crying 'Shit!' because, if truth be known, that was what he *really* wanted the sock to contain.

The run-through over, we would be joined by Wallace Greenslade, who, having finished his news reading duties for the day, acted as our announcer and linkman. Then the musicians would arrive, preceded by conductor Wally Stott, who always looked too frail to pick up his baton.

When the third series began in November 1952, The Ray Ellington Quartet and Max Geldray came into the show. By this time, the incomparable Peter Eton had taken over as producer. Peter would take no nonsense from any of us. I remember him having an argument with Peter Sellers about something or other, during which Sellers threatened to leave the show.

'All right,' said Eton. 'Bugger off then!' and Sellers, having started to leave the room, came back and sat down again.

He and Spike worked well together. Eton's work as a radio drama producer meant that he was prepared to experiment with sound effects – which was manna from heaven for Spike.

The two musical items from Ray Ellington and Max Geldray proved very popular. Ray was a huge success, not only because of his music but also because of his personality. It wasn't long before Spike was writing him into the script with exchanges like, 'Are you the colour sergeant?', to which the black Ellington would reply, 'Are you kidding?'. During the warm-up for the show Peter Sellers, no mean drummer himself, would join Ray on the bongos.

Max is a great jazz harmonica player. Dutch by birth, he now lives in Los Angeles, where he is a counsellor at the Betty Ford Clinic. It says a lot for his musicianship that his playing on the *Goon Show* tapes is still fresh today. Spike often put Max in the scripts with a Dutch expression or two. He was always referred to as 'Ploogie'. God knows why.

Anyway, back at the Camden Theatre, with the arrival of Ray and Max, we were ready for a run-through with effects and orchestra.

About this time, the pub next door to the theatre was always a welcome sight, and we would nip in for a couple before the recording proper. It was always full of friends of ours and Goon addicts, all of them would-be Bluebottles and Eccles and Neddies. Then it was back to the theatre, remembering to take a bottle of brandy and a pint of milk with us for the musical interludes – which might explain why the last part of the show was always so frenetic.

The warm-up for the show was sometimes funnier than

the show itself. It would begin with a 'jam session', with Peter playing the drums, Spike on trumpet and Wally Stott's session musicians – some of the best in the country.

Then Peter would announce that I was going to sing 'Falling in Love With Love', and while I was getting ready to sing, Spike would unclip the back of my braces without me knowing it.

I would then step forward, having already released the front buttons of my braces, and launch into the song. Along would come Spike, flexing his muscles. He would then put his hands up my jacket and pull my braces out. As he raised them aloft with a cry of triumph, I would get behind him and pull down his trousers.

One night, in an excess of zeal, I pulled down his underpants as well, eliciting a gasp from the audience followed by a round of applause which Milligan, a well built lad, gravely acknowledged before pulling his pants up.

After that lot of nonsense the *real* nonsense would begin as Wally Greenslade would ask for silence, wait for the green light and, with 'This is the BBC Home Service. Tiddly pong', we were off.

The only time the three of us appeared on stage together was at the Hippodrome in Coventry. It was the policy of the theatre to put on what they called a Birthday Show in the run-up to Christmas, and we were booked as the headliners.

I was to do my usual performance – a mixture of gags and straight songs; Spike was at that time still working on his act; and Peter, who was completely without nerves, was experimenting with all kinds of comic ideas because he hated doing the same act night after night. The only piece of material which we did together was a skit on Morris dancers (called the East Acton Stick Dancers) which Eric Sykes had written for one of my television shows. For this we wore farmers' smocks and shapeless hats and had bells round our ankles and waists. For some reason best known to himself, Peter appeared as a hunchback, à la Charles Laughton in the film *The Hunchback of Notre Dame*. We also carried sticks with bells attached, with which we bashed each other in time to the music of the 'Blue Bell Polka'.

One night Spike had a particularly bad reception from a bewildered audience and, after delivering the immortal line, 'I hope you all get bombed again,' he walked off to his dressing-room and locked the door. He could be heard from the corridor outside as he jumped up and down on his trumpet. After the interval, when the time came for him to join us on-stage for the East Acton Stick Dancers routine, he refused to leave his dressing-room.

Picture the scene as two grotesquely dressed idiots banged on his door, pleading with him to come out, our bells ringing merrily away while Sam Newsome, the theatre owner, the stage manager and the front of house manager wrung their hands in unison.

Meanwhile, in the auditorium, the restless citizens of Coventry started a slow hand clap.

Eventually, about fifteen minutes after the curtain should have gone up, a dishevelled and unrepentant Milligan responded to our pleading and emerged from his lair. We went on to do our act before a grim-faced audience.

After the performance, Spike was adamant that he was not going to continue with the show, but by the following day he relented and decided to stay on. The only snag was the fact that his trumpet, which was an essential part of his act, was flattened beyond repair and he had to borrow one from the pit orchestra. There were no recriminations from Peter or myself because we knew that Spike was going through a bad time with his manic depression, though I was beginning to think I might catch it off him.

One night, Peter went on stage armed with a chair and announced to the audience that he had been shopping that afternoon and had come across an EP recording of Wally Stott's orchestra playing a selection of Christmas songs. 'Having heard it,' he said, 'I was so delighted that I thought I'd like to share it with you.' He then gestured to the electrician in the sound box, whom he had previously briefed, and the theatre speakers resounded to a spirited rendering of 'God Rest You Merry Gentlemen'.

Peter then sat down centre stage on the chair that he had brought on, and rocked and swayed to the music, a beatific smile on his face.

The first side of the record completed, Peter stood up clapping, and the long-suffering folk out front joined in half-heartedly. 'I knew you'd like it!' he said, beaming at them. 'Let's have the other side.' And he sat down again as the Christmas music continued. When the EP was finished, he just picked up his chair and walked off with a cheery wave. I then had to follow this piece of stage magic with a slightly hysterical rendering of 'Bless This House'. This house was not very pleased.

Chaotic though it was, I thoroughly enjoyed the weeks in Coventry in the company of my anarchic friends – though I think the theatre management was glad to see the back of us.

The last *Goon Show* proper – 'The Last Smoking Seagoon' – went out in January 1960. But, twelve years later, in 1972, we were summoned back to record a special show as part of the BBC Silver Jubilee celebrations. The *Last Goon Show of All* was transmitted on 5 October 1972.

When we got together for the recording, which was done at our favourite studio, the Camden Theatre, we had not seen each other for a long while. I remember feeling quite nervous about the show and I wondered whether the old chemistry between us would still be there.

When I arrived at the theatre, I was greeted by John Browell, the producer of the last couple of series back in late

1959 and 1960.

'They're in the back room,' he said, referring to the small studio at the side of the theatre where we used to do our rehearsals for the show. Peter and Spike were indeed already in there, and after the excitement of meeting up again and the exchanging of reminiscences, we got down to reading the script. Initially, both Spike and Peter had difficulty in finding the voices of some of the characters. At first Peter could not get the right pitch for his Bluebottle, and Spike had a spot of bother with his famous Eccles. I was all right because Neddy Seagoon was my normal voice, pitched a few decibels louder.

There was one sad note. Wally Greenslade, who had taken over the part of the announcer from Andrew Timothy from the start of the fifth series in September 1954 right up to the end, had since died, but it was great to have Andrew Timothy back for this special show. Ray Ellington was there too, and Max Geldray had flown in specially from the States.

By the time we had read the script through, the old timing began to come back and we were all more relaxed. Peter was now a really big star and I had wondered whether he would be the same old Pete of ten years ago. I need not have worried and soon the years fell away as we tried our characters on for size.

There could not have been a greater contrast between this *Last Goon Show of All* and the early ones. In the audience that night were Prince Philip, Princess Margaret, Lord Snowdon and Princess Anne. Unfortunately, our greatest royal admirer, Prince Charles, was unable to attend, but had sent a very funny telegram regretting his absence.

I first met Prince Charles at a luncheon at Lancaster House prior to his Investiture and it was then that I found out that he was an avid *Goon Show* follower. We discussed important matters of state, such as what was the Welsh word for 'chips' and I asked his equerry, Squadron Leader David Checketts, if HRH would like to meet Spike and Peter. He said he was sure that he would be delighted to do so.

Eventually a date was fixed and Prince Charles and Checketts drove down from Cambridge together to have lunch with the three of us at Peter Sellers's house in Elstead, Surrey, where he lived in some style. It was a most memorable meal during which the young Prince revealed an astonishing knowledge of past Goon Shows and an uncanny ability to imitate most of the characters. I remember saying at the time that if anything happened to the Royal family he could join us, a case of 'Heir today and Goon tomorrow'. He laughed and said, 'It's very draughty in the Tower these days, Ned.'

Myra, my eldest daughter Jennifer and I were lucky enough to be invited to the Investiture Ball at Caernarvon Castle and on the drive up there we were listening to the ceremony being broadcast on the radio. The newly invested Prince of Wales was making his speech in Welsh and I happened to hear the word 'Goon' mentioned. I said to Myra 'I didn't know that there was a Welsh word "Goon", I wonder what it means?' Then when he repeated his speech in English I realized what he was saying. He said that 'Wales had produced many a poet, tragedian and a most memorable Goon.' I nearly drove the car off the road.

'I wonder what the historians of the future will make of that?' I said proudly.

'Never mind about them,' said Myra. 'Keep your eyes on the road.' Phlegmatic some Welsh people are indeed.

When we arrived at the Castle we found ourselves in the midst of hundreds of Welsh singers and I sang myself hoarse with my mates Geraint Evans and Stuart Burrows. It was a night to remember but I'm afraid that I imbibed a little too much Welsh ale and I honestly cannot do so. Myra said I enjoyed myself and I'll take her word for it. It was a good job I didn't have to drive home until the next morning.

The next day I sent a cable to HRH in Malta saying

'Thanks for the free plug. Milligan and Sellers are clamouring for Welsh citizenship.' He took the time to write a very funny letter in reply which I shall be proud to pass on to my children.

Back in 1951 we had been four young comics determined to change the face of comedy one way or another – iconoclasts and rebels, chopping away at the feet of the establishment of which we were now a part. It is a typical characteristic of the British hierarchy that it absorbs its rebels and makes them respectable. Makarios in Cyprus and Jomo Kenyatta both came to power after leading revolutions. Milligan might yet be Prime Minister.

The *Last Goon Show of All* went down extremely well with the studio audience, and the appearance of favourite characters such as Bluebottle and Eccles was greeted with rapturous applause. But, to be honest, it was by no means a vintage show, and the presence of Royalty out front lent a kind of reverence to what should have been an irreverent occasion.

However, it was great to be back in harness again working with two wayward geniuses. It was a pity that Mike Bentine had not been invited back for this last show. As a founder member of the Goons, he should have been with us at the finish.

Radio Days

I was involved in a lot of radio programmes in the early fifties of which *Welsh Rarebit* was one. This was produced by Mac Jones and came from Corey Hall in Cardiff. The closing song of the programme was 'We'll Keep a Welcome' which eventually became part of my stage repertoire.

There were two radio series in those days which also helped my career. They were produced by Pat Dixon who pioneered the *Goon Show* and were very advanced comedy shows for their time. One was called *Listen My Children* and the other was *Third Division*, both containing material by Muir and Norden.

I joined the cast of *Educating Archie* in 1953. The radio series featured the ventriloquist Peter Brough and his dummy Archie Andrews, and I took over the role of Archie's tutor from Tony Hancock. It was an amazingly popular show at the time – especially considering that the central character was a wooden doll!

Edgar Bergen had broken new ground in America when he did a radio programme with his famous dummies Charlie McCarthy and Mortimer Snerd. (Incidentally, the voice of

Mortimer Snerd became much imitated in radio programmes as the quintessential 'idiot', and was adopted by Spike in a slightly different form for his Eccles character in the *Goon Show*.) However, a strong cast had been built up around Archie. Max Bygraves and Julie Andrews were in the first series, which was written by Eric Sykes and Sid Colin. Tony Hancock had joined the team for the second series as Archie's tutor, and started to make a big name for himself. Beryl Reid, Hattie Jacques and myself were the newcomers to the team, and I stayed until the end of the fourth series in April 1954. I was also doing the *Goon Show* during most of this time, rehearsing and recording both programmes on the same Sunday. In between times I managed to squeeze in an hour's singing lesson.

Eric, Max and I became great mates – we had all been in the services and had the same sense of humour, which was not always shared by Peter Brough.

I remember one particular Sunday when the three of us came back late from our lunch break. We had been held up in a restaurant around the corner from the Paris Cinema in Lower Regent Street where we recorded the show. Brough was furious with us and gave us a good ticking off, which we resented because the delay was not our fault. We sulked a bit and then decided that we would somehow get our own back on the following Sunday.

I don't remember exactly whose idea it was to play a trick on Brough by doing something to Archie when his master wasn't looking, but I think it was Eric's.

Peter's usual routine was to walk on stage first from behind the curtains which hid the cast from the audience, leaving Archie sitting on a stool to await being picked up and presented to his fans out front. This meant that we had the dummy to ourselves for a minute or two while Peter started the warm-up. Max had brought a red rubber glove from home, and we quickly stuffed it into Archie's little trousers, opening the buttons on his flies and leaving one finger sticking out. We had just finished doing this when Peter came back behind the curtains to snatch up the now tumescent little Archie, not noticing that he had been tampered with.

We waited for the reaction from the audience.

'Hello, Archie,' said Peter, his lips moving behind his cigar as he settled the dummy on his knee.

There was a moment of shocked silence as the audience took in Archie's condition. This was followed by some stifled laughter and a shriek from Peter when he discovered what had been done to his dummy. He raced back to the safety of the curtains, red-faced with embarrassment. It was obvious to him who the culprits were, but to give him his credit he took the joke very well.

Peter might not have had a great sense of humour, but he did have a good sense of injustice. During the series I had been given a song to sing in each programme, which meant that I had to leave the microphone into which I spoke my dialogue and rush over to another one near the orchestra for the song. Quite often this left me out of breath at the beginning of the song with the consequence that I occasionally strayed off the note. This was the cause of some complaints from listeners with finer-tuned musical sensibilities than I possessed and led to the Head of BBC Radio Variety, Michael Standing, banning me from singing solos in future shows.

To his eternal credit, Peter stood up for me and through his musical associate, Wally Ridley, who was then the recording manager of HMV, I was introduced to the man who ultimately saved my singing career – Manlio di Veroli, an Italian singing teacher.

Manlio took my voice apart like an expert mechanic strips down an engine. He lived in a flat at the back of Marble Arch and had a remarkable history. He had trained at the Academy of St Cecilia in Rome at the same time as Gigli. As a very young boy he had met Verdi, and he had been chorus master for

Puccini. He employed the famous bel-canto technique, using the diaphragm as a bellows, giving the singer greater control over his voice, carrying the sound up through the chest and into the head cavities and preventing too much strain on the vocal chords.

To reach Manlio's flat, I had to climb a very steep staircase, at the top of which was a door that led into his studio, where a grand piano filled the room. There were dozens of photographs on top of the piano, all signed by famous singers – Chaliapin, for whom Manlio had been accompanist at many concerts, expressed his eternal gratitude for Manlio's help; Gigli declared his affection; Valente, a fine operatic tenor who had recorded *Turandot* under the baton of my new maestro, thanked him profusely for his assistance.

In another room, Manlio's devoted wife, Selma, would be preparing spaghetti sauce for the evening meal, and it was difficult to stop salivating at the very aroma of her cooking.

My first task, after I had recovered my breath from the climb up to his studio, was to run through a few scales, and the rest of the lesson would be concerned with interpreting a phrase or two of 'Caro mio ben', an aria by Gluck which requires a tremendous amount of breath control. I would be dying to let rip with a bit of 'Vesti la giubba', or one of Mario Lanza's belters, but Manlio very firmly and sensibly confined me to singing only those things that would improve my technique.

It took years of sacrifice on my part – driving down from northern towns after the second house on a Saturday night to be in Marble Arch for a lesson with the maestro on the Sunday morning, prior to a *Goon Show* rehearsal, and then driving back early on the Monday morning for another band call in another town.

Manlio insisted that I took opera seriously and had a fervent desire to see me on stage at Covent Garden. 'Give up these Goons,' he would say. 'You can earn hundreds and pounds with the voice.'

I refrained from telling him that I was already earning 'hundreds and pounds' in Variety, but part of me wanted to believe him.

'Please don't go cross-eyed in the middle of the aria, Harry,' he'd say, half-jokingly. 'Puccini was up all night writing it.'

I remember him ringing me up after a record of mine was played on *Housewives' Choice* one morning. 'You sang better today, Harry,' he said.

The result of my first course of lessons was that my voice improved tremendously – so much so that when *Educating Archie* won the *Daily Mail* Top Variety Series Award at the Scala Theatre in February 1953, I was allowed to sing 'Vesti la giubba' on the programme. I had Peter Brough to thank for that and, to my surprise, *I* also received the thanks of Michael Standing, who complimented me on my performance. I felt good that night.

One Sunday at the *Goon Show* rehearsals at the Camden Theatre, I received a frantic telephone call from Dennis Main Wilson, who was calling from the Paris Cinema Studio. 'Can you come down here and take over *Hancock's Half Hour*? It's the beginning of the second series and he hasn't turned up.' Tony had apparently walked out following a disagreement with the management of a show he was appearing in at the Adelphi and couldn't be found anywhere. Dennis, who was the producer of the Hancock show, had already spoken to my agent and to the producer of the *Goon Show*, both of whom had agreed to alter the rehearsal schedules to accommodate my doing the two shows.

I knew Tony Hancock well, but I also knew that his timing and delivery were different from mine, and before I read the Ray Galton and Alan Simpson script I was afraid that it might not work as well with me in a role that had been tailor made for Tony. As it turned out, the script was so beautifully written and the supporting cast of Sid James, Bill Kerr and Kenneth Williams was so strong in performance that anyone could have done it.

I did two more shows – this time with scripts written for me – and I was enjoying myself in the part, although it was still announced as '*Hancock's Half Hour* featuring Harry Secombe'.

On the Monday following the broadcast of the third programme, Tony unexpectedly appeared at the stage door of a theatre I was playing in Shrewsbury. He came into my dressing-room and apologized for his absence. I didn't think it was right to ask him where he'd been and he didn't offer any explanation. After he had thanked me for holding the fort he drove off in his green Jaguar.

The following Sunday, Galton and Simpson wrote a special opening piece in which I handed over to Tony – and away he went.

It was a real pleasure to perform those three scripts and when, after the second one, Dennis Main Wilson hinted that perhaps I could take over the series, I admit I was tempted. But Tony was an old friend and I had enough on my plate with the *Goon Show*, so that was that.

Anyone who does a job of work and at the end of the day has nothing tangible to show for it, apart from his salary, has every reason to feel insecure. This is perhaps particularly true of show business – you can't frame applause, you can't place cheers on your mantelpiece and you can't plant a chuckle in a pot and expect it to raise laughs. All the average comic is left with at the end of his career are some yellowing newspaper cuttings, perhaps an LP or two and a couple of lines in *The Stage* obituary column. But, if he is one of the few greats, he leaves behind a legacy of laughter when he has gone, especially, it seems, if there was an element of tragedy in his life.

Tony Hancock was one of those rare ones who are bedevilled by success. He was never completely happy in the

Variety theatre; the strain of repeating the same performance night after night and trying to invest it with apparent spontaneity was more than he could bear. His timing and delivery were never better than when he was doing something fresh – creating and not recreating. That was why he took to television so well, it took him from the treadmill of the music hall and gave him new situations in which to work his magic.

Of the rampaging, drunken, self-destroying Hancock depicted in so many stories, I knew very little. I had drunk with him and been drunk with him in the days when we were both young and inexperienced comics fresh from the services, but it was all good-natured tippling then. The truth we were searching for wasn't far away – it was there in the bottom of the glass.

The time I remember Tony with most affection was when we were playing on the same bill at Feldman's Theatre, Blackpool in April 1949. I was doing my shaving act, in which I simply demonstrated the different ways people shave, and Tony was doing his Gaumont British News impressions and some hesitant patter. On the opening night – Monday 11 April – I was rushed to the manager's office to receive a telephone call telling me that Myra had just given birth to our baby daughter, Jennifer. I waited until Tony came off and told him the news. 'We'll celebrate, lad!' he cried.

With twelve shillings between us and it being too late to get to the pub, we ended up in a fish and chip shop with rock salmon and Tizer. Later, we wandered down to the sea front and argued about what we would do with the world now we had fought to save it, leaning over the iron bars of the promenade, looking into the dark sea and seeing only brightness.

I will always think of Tony Hancock as he was then – pristine and shining with ambition at the threshold of his career. The demands of his profession shaped him, ground him down and eventually killed him, but he served it well.

If anyone paid dearly for his laughs, it was the lad himself.

Treading the Boards

'I'm going fishing, love,' I said to Myra.

'Be careful on those rocks, now.'

'Don't worry,' I replied. 'I'm wearing my guaranteed non-slip American sports shoes.'

This exchange – somewhat fateful as it turned out – took place at the Ariel Sands Hotel in Bermuda at Easter in 1956. Myra and I had just come back from New York where I had been appearing on the *Ed Sullivan Show*. It had been a hectic time, so we were spending a few quiet days in Bermuda on the way back to London and my first starring role at the Palladium in *Rocking the Town*.

'Relax and enjoy yourselves,' was the advice of my agent, Jimmy Grafton.

I had read somewhere that fishing was a great way to relax, and according to the Ariel Sands' brochure there was great sport to be had off the rocks in front of the hotel.

And so it was with great expectations that I sallied forth from our bungalow, festooned with fishing equipment and head held high – which turned out to be a mistake, because I tripped over a large piece of coral. The sight of a corpulent tourist sprawled on the sand was too much for a group of local children who began jumping around with glee. After I had managed to sort myself out, they decided to follow me and see what further entertainment was in store.

I was reminded of the time on the beach at Cap d'Antibes when I was mistaken for ex-King Farouk, who happened to be staying in the area. Some French kids elected to walk behind me, pointing and giggling, until I turned around and gave them a fruity raspberry. This unregal action convinced them that I was not the man they thought I was and they reluctantly dispersed.

Unfortunately the same tactic only seemed to increase the mirth of the Bermudian children, so I decided to find a place on the rocks which was as far away as possible from my new 'fan club'. They still followed my scrambled progress for a while, until a swimmer in difficulty off to my left, presented a better opportunity for merriment and they drifted away.

I was now able to concentrate on my fishing. The sea was calm and I made my first cast in high anticipation. Unfortunately, the hook snagged on an underwater rock about ten feet out and no amount of tugging would free it. I realized I would have to swim out to retrieve it.

There was a nice flat rock just in front of me from which I could launch myself into the sea. However, the moment I put my foot on it I lost my balance and fell. In order to break my fall I stretched out my left arm, with the result that the bone snapped. It went off like a pistol shot and when I eventually got to my feet in my guaranteed 'non-slip' American rubber shoes, my arm hung uselessly at my side. I could move my fingers but that was all.

'I open at the Palladium in three weeks' time,' I thought, as I trudged painfully back to the hotel, leaving the equipment behind. On the way I met some of the lads who had enjoyed my earlier antics. 'You missed the best bit,' I said through gritted teeth.

The return flight to London was a turbulent one, and every

jolt went through my freshly plastered arm like a knife. The doctor who treated me in the hospital in Hamilton said that I really should have an aeroplane splint with my arm sticking out at a right angle to my body, but I persuaded him that I could not possibly perform on stage like that. So, against his better judgement, he plastered the arm with my elbow bent, and bound it in a cocoon of crêpe bandages across my chest. At least my hand was free.

'Juggling is definitely out, but you can still sing,' said Myra, comfortingly.

Rehearsals for the Palladium began in earnest when I got back. An excellent cast had been gathered together, some members of which I had already had the pleasure of working with previously.

Beryl Reid was an old mate from *Educating Archie* and I was delighted to learn that we would be working together in sketches. Beryl has a tremendous sense of humour and a wicked wit and is one of the few Variety stars to make it big as a character actress. Whenever we worked together at the Palladium, she took great pains to make sure that the clothes she wore were exactly right for the part. She always said that the secret of finding the right clothes was to begin with the shoes. Once she felt that her feet were comfortably settled, the rest was easy. The lovely singer Alma Cogan was also in the show and Winifred Attwell – along with her two pianos – completed the female line-up.

Eric Rogers was the conductor of the orchestra. He and I went back a long way. He was a Swansea boy, and his brother Alan had been in the Swansea Territorial Regiment in which I had served. Eric and I often walked to school together down Morris Lane – a very steep hill which led down from the Grenfell Park Road estate, where we both lived, to the road which crossed the East Dock bridge and was the main thoroughfare into Swansea town.

Eric could play nearly every instrument in the orchestra and in addition to being a fine conductor, he was an extremely talented arranger and composer, providing the music for most of the *Carry On* films and many other, more serious, epics. He was later to arrange Lionel Bart's music for the film of *Oliver!* in which I would play Mr Bumble, the Beadle.

It was very reassuring to find that I had a friend in the orchestra pit, because I usually found myself somewhat inhibited in the presence of musicians, mainly owing to my lack of formal musical training and a tendency to stray from the note when under pressure.

The main supporting acts on the Palladium bill were The Cinq Peres, a very funny French singing act, Gene Detroy's performing chimpanzees and an amazing young juggler called Rudy Horn.

The first time any of us saw Rudy's act was at the dress rehearsal. I was sitting in the stalls with Charles Henry, who was responsible for the comedy production of the show, a man with a legendary dry sense of humour. It was he who, when asked how well *Goodnight Vienna* would do in Walthamstow, replied 'About as well as *Goodnight Walthamstow* would do in Vienna.'

On to the stage on a unicycle rode Rudy Horn, dressed in short pants and knee-length white socks, accompanied, on foot, by a sequin-clad lady (who, it transpired, was his mother). It was her task to throw various articles to Rudy which he would then balance on his head, nose or chin, while he simultaneously circled the stage on one wheel.

The climax of his act was truly staggering. One by one he tossed up from his foot on to his head, six saucers and cups. When they were all balanced in position, he flicked up a spoon which landed in the top saucer. Then, as if that was not enough, his mother placed a lump of sugar on his toe and up it flew to land in the top cup.

The audience of performers watching from the stalls burst

into spontaneous applause and loud cheers. But not Charlie. He sat alongside me, shaking his head.

'What's up, Charles?' I was amazed at his lack of enthusiasm.

'He's not as good as he used to be.'

'What do you mean?' I asked.

He sucked his teeth reflectively before replying. 'He used to use demerara.'

During the try-out at the Birmingham Hippodrome I was experiencing such discomfort with my plastered arm that I made a morning appointment with Sir Osmond Clarke, a noted bone specialist, at the London Clinic.

When he cut the cocoon of bandages away he discovered that the lime in the plaster had burned into the flesh on my side. 'You poor man,' he said. 'We'll have to do something about this.' He then made a phone call to a colleague who came down to see the damage that the plaster had done.

'Try some Mycil ointment on that,' was his colleague's advice.

After he had left I said to 'Nobby' Clarke, ' I think I've met him somewhere before.'

'That's Archibald McIndoe, the man who helped all those airmen who were so badly burned in the war.' He started cutting away the plaster as he spoke.

'Of course, I did a show for his "guinea pigs" at East Grinstead Hospital,' I managed to say just before I passed out.

After my arm had been re-set and pads of soothing Mycil ointment placed between the plaster and my ribs, I caught a train back to Birmingham and was at the theatre in time for the first performance.

The producer of the show was the legendary Robert Nesbitt and to be honest I was slightly in awe of him. He was always immaculately dressed in a dark suit and always wore a tie and a shirt with snowy white cuffs.

When rehearsals began on the stage proper – we would go through our paces in different bars around the theatre – he always had a work space towards the back of the stalls, which consisted of a wooden trestle table laid over two rows of seats. On it he would have a couple of telephones, a bottle of champagne in an ice bucket and all the paraphernalia of music scores and lighting plots, etc., together with a mike through which he would issue instructions to the stage-manager, the redoubtable, unshakeable Jack Matthews.

Robert was most meticulous about his lighting and would spend what to some would seem an inordinate amount of time getting the effect he wanted. There is a story that once, during a break in rehearsals, a stage-hand went to pick up a pot of paint that was sitting centre stage. 'Don't touch that,' said Jack Matthews. 'Mr Nesbitt's just spent two hours lighting it.'

Sometimes, in his search for perfection, Robert would become irritable and raise his voice. That usually got results. 'But I don't *understand*, dear boy,' he would call out in exasperation, and some poor stage-hand would fear for his life.

There was one occasion in the early hours of the morning during a last dress rehearsal, when everything seemed to be going wrong. His telephone rang loudly and because Ros, his secretary, was elsewhere at the time, he answered the call himself.

'Yes, what is it?' he said, bringing the proceedings on stage to a halt.

It was Maude, the wife of Len Lightowler, who was my manager at that time. 'What time will Harry be home for his supper?' said Maude in her strong Yorkshire accent. 'We've got steak and kidney pie for him and Myra wants to know when to put it in the oven.'

Robert stood silently for a moment with the phone to his ear. 'I don't know,' he said with something like a whimper. 'I honestly don't know.' And sat down.

Once I got to know him better, I realized that he had a good sense of humour and was an excellent dinner companion. He has left us now and, after he died, it was said with affection by one of his friends that Robert's first job upstairs would be to re-light the Pearly Gates.

Rocking the Town opened on 17 May 1956 and, to everyone's relief, it was a triumph. I thought the best way to deal with the broken arm was to draw attention to it at the beginning of the show and then carry on as normal.

I made my first entrance in a lift which came down from the flies disguised as a dressing-room door bearing a bright golden star. It came down quite fast and then just a couple of feet from the ground it slowed down to land me gently on to the stage. I opened the door and stepped out to a gratifyingly warm reception from the audience.

'It's always been my ambition to play the Palladium with a huge supporting cast – and here it is,' I announced, tapping my plastered arm. 'It doesn't bother me any more – and I hope it won't bother you.' And off we went . . .

They were a wonderful audience that night and the whole evening's entertainment was received with great enthusiasm. I finished the show with the aria 'E lucevan le stelle' from *Tosca*, wearing what I used to call my 'singing suit' – a white silk shirt and a pair of black trousers. I sang it as well as I had ever done – for Myra's benefit as well as my reputation.

During the applause that followed, Myra turned to her friend Maude with tears in her eyes. 'Look at him up there,' she said, 'and I have to wash his crutty underpants.'

Nineteen-fifty-six was a big year for me, as it also featured the most memorable Royal Command Performance in which I've been invited to perform: the one that never was. It was the fifth of November – Guy Fawkes Night, the traditional time for fireworks in England, but unfortunately the biggest bangs were going off elsewhere – in Hungary, where the

Russian tanks were brutally quelling the revolution, and in Egypt where the British and the French were attempting to overthrow Nasser and take control of the Suez Canal. Not an altogether propitious time to set a jolly dish of variety ingredients before a Queen.

Val Parnell had assembled a tremendous array of talent to perform at the London Palladium that year. Liberace and his brother George were among the American headliners, along with Jerry Colonna, who appeared in many Bob Hope films. Antonio, the famous Spanish flamenco dancer, was also on the bill, along with home-grown performers such as Max Bygraves, Bud Flanagan, Beryl Reid, Jimmy Wheeler and myself among many others. As I was the incumbent of the number one dressing-room for the summer season, I was only too delighted to act as host to some of the visiting performers.

The number one dressing-room consisted of two adjoining rooms, both of which opened into the corridor. Liberace and his brother had been allotted the make-up room, which was divided by a door from the reception room which Max Bygraves and I shared. I had stacked enough booze in our room to satisfy the most demanding drinkers in the business – of which Jimmy Wheeler was the greatest – but it was all being kept in a locked cupboard until after the show.

Those of us who had already done our band rehearsal gathered in the stalls to watch the other acts going through their paces with the orchestra. Some used the resident conductor while the American artists had brought over their own.

It is always a great thrill for me to watch some of the legendary names in the profession doing a band call, to hear the banter between the act on stage and the musicians in the pit. On these special occasions we are all in the same boat – the famous performers and the most humble 'wines and spirits' acts share the same nervousness about the approaching show, knowing that the star of the evening is going to be the Queen, who will never *ever* be upstaged. With this knowledge in mind, there is a humility in even the most temperamental members of our business.

I happened to be sitting next to Jimmy Wheeler when Antonio the flamenco dancer came on stage. The Spaniard was wearing a very tight-fitting pair of trousers and a bolero-style jacket, and as he drummed his heels and twisted and turned to the rhythm of his musicians, Jimmy leaned over to me. 'One can of beans and he'd ruin that bloody suit,' he said.

We were about halfway through the dress rehearsal when I was called into the bar at the rear of the stalls. Val Parnell had sent for Bud Flanagan and a few other members of the cast, including myself, because he had something very important to ask us. We gathered around him as he told us that he had just received a call from Buckingham Palace saying that Her Majesty had been advised not to attend the performance because the seriousness of the international situation made it inadvisable.

When Val had given us the news, he wanted our opinion about whether or not the show should go on without the Queen in attendance. It was unanimously agreed that a Royal Command Performance without the Queen being present was definitely out of the question.

Val then went on stage and declared to a hushed and hastily assembled cast that the show was cancelled. There was a stunned reaction from everyone present. Some of the acts were in tears – Liberace in particular, was inconsolable, and he and George shut themselves in their room.

Meanwhile, next door, I decided the time was right to open up the drinks cupboard and drown everybody's sorrows. Beryl Reid and Alma Cogan came in, along with Jerry Colonna, Jimmy Wheeler, Max Bygraves and Eric Sykes – who had dropped in to watch the rehearsal. In no time at all the room was packed with people, while poor Liberace languished next door.

'Come on out,' we pleaded, banging on the door. Eventually he came out to join us and I have the bizarre recollection of Max, Eric and myself standing around him and joining in with Jimmy Wheeler as the comedian went into his routine: 'If you have to get a boil, get a big 'un, and we can all sit round and watch it throb . . .'

This certainly cheered up Liberace, but I don't think he understood a word of it. The rest of the evening was a bit kaleidoscopic but I do know that I arrived home at 129 Cheam Road to a grateful Myra and the kids just in time to let off the fireworks in the garden. In the process I managed to burn a big hole in my white polo-neck sweater, but it got a laugh from the children, so the evening wasn't entirely wasted.

While we are on the subject of Royal Command Performances, 1958 was another one I will never forget. It was at the London Coliseum and the artists included The Beverley Sisters, Frankie Vaughan, Bruce Forsyth, Pat Boone, Eartha Kitt, to name but a few.

The soprano Adele Leigh and I were to sing the famous 'Misere' duet from *Il Trovatore*. Mantovani and his orchestra were to accompany us, and with my customary caution I had asked for the pianist in the pit to give me a bell note so that I'd be able to enter in tune. Adele, of course, had no such difficulty with pitch, having sung the opera many times. Had Adele been the one to begin the duet there would have been no problem, but the sight of Mantovani wincing during rehearsals at my effort to find the note, was enough for me to fix it with the pit pianist.

When it came to the actual performance I stood confidently as the orchestra played the introduction. 'Bom-diddy bom, tiddy bom tiddy bom' they went, while I waited for my note. It never came. I waited for an 'A' but the pianist had gone for a pee. Subsequently I came in half-a-tone sharp, but luckily Adele came to my rescue and got me back on track.

I was forcibly reminded of the time when I sang 'Granada'

on a *Goon Show* recording. When I had finished, Stanley Black, the conductor, hissed at me 'Do you realize that you sang that tune a quarter of a tone sharp all the way through?'

I turned to him and replied, 'Do you think that's easy?'

He threw his baton at me.

But the real reason that the 1958 Royal Command Performance was so unforgettable was because it was one of those rare occasions when an unknown performer became the hit of the show.

I was doing a spot of compèring that night and I was in the wings to watch the act that preceded the one I was to announce. What I saw was a young bespectacled lad who took the bejewelled, dinner-jacketed audience by the throat and had them yelling for more. He danced, he sang, he played the trumpet and he told a few jokes – and they wouldn't let him go.

He came off stage to where I was waiting, his eyes wide in disbelief at what was happening to him. I had to push him back three times to take a bow before the audience would let him leave the stage, and Roy Castle became a star that night. I little knew then how much he would enrich my life, or how interwoven our families would become.

And many years after, when he was battling his cancer and appeared on stage for his last few performances in *Pickwick*, and I used to bring him down to the front of the stage at the end of the show for a special bow, there was that same look of disbelief in his eyes as the audience rose to its feet in an outpouring of love.

I feel privileged that I was there at the very beginning and at the triumphant though tragic end of his brilliant career.

Another memorable Royal Command was the one in November 1963. At the time I was appearing at the Saville Theatre in *Pickwick* and impresario Bernard Delfont wanted a couple of songs from the show for the Royal performance which was held at the Prince of Wales Theatre. It was a big cast which included Marlene Dietrich and the young lads who had recently become the nation's darlings, The Beatles.

I was standing on stage during a break in rehearsals when Marlene's dresser, who it turned out later was her daughter, came to me and said that Miss Dietrich would like to meet The Beatles. As I had met the boys on a couple of occasions, I brought them across to her. They didn't seem to be all that impressed to be meeting her, though she turned the full battery of her charm on them. Looking back, I had no idea that I had brought two great world legends together for one brief moment. The show business equivalent of Stanley meeting Livingstone, marred only by the fact that I didn't know all the boys' names.

That was the night when The Beatles told the glittering audience to 'rattle their jewellery'.

In the finale I had to come forward and call for three cheers for Her Majesty. Just before I did so, I took off my bald wig and put it on backwards, with the grey fringe of hair now in front, saying: 'Look folks, The Beatles in fifty years' time!' It went down quite well for an ad lib and must have made some kind of lasting impression because years later at a charity dinner, Princess Margaret reminded me of it.

'Why did you do it?' she asked.

I could not think of a reply.

My second Palladium revue was *Large as Life*, which opened on 23 May 1958.

Val Parnell was still Managing Director of the Palladium and Bernard Delfont was also on the management side. Once again, Robert Nesbitt was the producer and George Carden was the choreographer. The cast consisted of a lot of my old mates – Terry-Thomas, Eric Sykes, Hattie Jacques and Harry Worth.

This time there was a theme, of sorts, to the show. The first half was all about the world of the theatre going from a Harlequinade to the days of Music Hall. This gave Robert Nesbitt the opportunity to bring on some music hall veterans to close the first act. Hetty King, G H Elliot and Dick Henderson – Dickie's father – all came on to do their party pieces and proved that they could still bring the audiences to their feet.

The second half was concerned with the world of revue and Eric, Hattie, Harry Worth and I did a burlesque of *The Three Musketeers*. But the loudest laughs came for Johnny Puleo and His Harmonica Rascals. Johnny was a Punchinello-type dwarf who had taken over Borrah Minevitch's Harmonica Rascals, an act that had often featured in American film musicals. Johnny was a great little man and I never failed to watch him from the wings – there was a lot to learn from the way he handled his comedy.

There was also a lot to learn from Hetty, Dick and G H Elliot. On the first night, as the curtains came down on the finale, all the cast left the stage as the orchestra played the National Anthem – except for the three old-timers, who stood to attention as the 'Queen' was played. I saw this and felt ashamed and on the second night I joined them. The third night saw the whole company on parade until the orchestra had finished.

Eric had written some very funny sketches for the show including the Marching routine he had worked out for my first ITV comedy show. Another idea of his was the Top Graders, a burlesque of an American pop group in which we were joined by Max Russell, who often worked as a straight man in shows with me.

Harry Worth had gone down so well in the Variety season at the Palladium in the weeks preceding our show that Bernard Delfont kept him on. It was the first time that Harry had ever worked in sketches and he was most apprehensive at rehearsals. When I started to give him a big build-up before his act, he appeared from the wings, quite upset. Shading his eyes from the front spotlight with his hand, he called out to Robert Nesbitt who was in his usual place in the stalls watching the rehearsal. 'Please Mr Nesbitt,' said Harry, 'I can't possibly follow that. I like to come on quietly and cull the laughs.'

So all I said to introduce him was 'Ladies and Gentlemen – Harry Worth' and he took it from there with great effect.

Terry-Thomas was making a film at the same time as appearing at the Palladium and travelled in a private ambulance from the studios to the theatre. He had been placed in the second half of the show to give him a bit of extra time. After his solo act he joined Eric, Hattie, Harry and me in the *Three Musketeers* burlesque. Terry was not unknown to have a drink or two during the day and some nights we had to hold him up during the fencing scene that closed the sketch. He was a great giggler and he used to set off the rest of us, which sometimes puzzled the second house audiences who didn't know what we were laughing at.

Very unprofessional behaviour, I'm afraid, but we enjoyed ourselves. After the show, Terry, Eric, Harry and others would gather in my dressing-room and Terry would keep us in hysterics with his 'shaggy dog' stories. He had the gift of making the run up as funny as the end of the gag itself.

Every Saturday, between the second and third perform-ances, I used to send up a bottle of champagne to G H Elliot's dressing-room for the three veterans to share. They always appreciated it and I was thanked most politely and formally by the three of them individually. G H would save the cork for applying his 'black face' make-up, a ritual he kept secret, and I don't think he was ever approached about the subject by any member of the cast. We all had a great deal of respect for the old-timers because they had all been top of the bill in their day. At times, I felt it was very sad that they had to spend their declining years still working thirteen shows a week, when they should have been enjoying the fruits of their labour in contented retirement. I don't know whether they were reluctant to give up appearing on stage or whether they were forced to do so for financial reasons.

Now that I am in my seventies and find myself doing exactly the same thing as they did, I think I know how they felt. Although I am fortunate enough to be still playing the lead in *Pickwick*, there is a reluctance in me to leave the spotlight and retire to the safety of the wings, leaving the stage for younger, more able actors to take over. Sometimes on a matinée day when I'm doing *Pickwick*, the thought of not having to go out and face another audience ever again is decidedly appealing and I sink lower into the armchair in my dressing-room savouring the thought. Then the orchestra starts up and the voice over the tannoy calls 'Overtures and beginners' and, like an old war-horse scenting the battlefield, I am up on my feet with a last look in the mirror and off down the stairs to the stage, adrenalin pumping away, and there's nowhere else that I want to be.

Yes, I think I know now how they felt.

I have always found pantomime the most difficult type of show to work in. When you are sitting in your dressing-room before curtain up, the loudspeaker on the wall relays the roar of the children's chatter and you wonder whether your voice will last the performance.

It's a battle, folks.

When you do make your entrance, the reek of wet knickers and oranges assaults the nostrils.

But a Palladium pantomime is a different thing. The scenery and costumes are always magnificent and most of the music is original.

In December 1959, I opened in the best panto I ever appeared in. *Humpty Dumpty* was the last panto Val Parnell presented before embarking on his television career. Robert

Nesbitt was in the producer's chair once again, and the lyrics and music were specially written for the show by David Croft and Cyril Ornadel.

It was a change from the traditional pantomime because there was no principal boy – well, there was, but he really *was* a boy. Gary Miller played Tommy Tucker and Stephanie Voss was Mistress Mary. There was no Dame and the story was set firmly in the land of nursery rhyme. Four days before we opened, Sally Smith, who was to play Mistress Mary, had appendicitis and Stephanie Voss stepped in to fill the breach. It was a great tribute to Stephanie that she was word perfect on opening night. Alfred Marks and Paddy O'Neill were the King and Queen of Hearts and Roy Castle was Simple Simon.

I had not really seen much of Roy since the night he took the Royal Command Performance audience by storm the previous year. He had been given his own TV show, which had received an unfair drubbing by some critics, and when we started the rehearsals he was feeling pretty low. However, as the days went by his confidence began to return and when we finally opened his routine as a clown, in which he did not say a word, was one of the funniest things in the show. He soon put his TV troubles behind him and from then on his professional career zoomed into orbit.

It was a very spectacular production and the critics were lavish in their praise for Robert Nesbitt. I remember one particular piece of stage magic which I watched from the stalls at the dress rehearsal. At the end of the first act there was a pageant of the four seasons which ended in a fantastic snow fall and Santa Claus in a real sledge made an entry aloft which came alive with twinkling lights as the orchestra played 'I'm Dreaming of a White Christmas'. The effect on those of us who saw it was electrifying. I don't believe I have ever been moved so much in the theatre. Why, I don't really know, but the combination of 'White Christmas' and the appearance of Santa in his sleigh epitomized the magic of Christmas.

Even the broadsheet critics, who have not always seen eye to eye with me, were effusive in their praise. Philip Hope-Wallace in the *Guardian* said: 'This is the pantomime for me. Not for years have I seen the title role so perfectly cast . . .' 'The Palladium's "*Humpty Dumpty*" triumphantly blends pageantry and fun in a way that Christmas spectaculars in the West End rarely achieve,' wrote Richard Findlater in the *Observer*, going on to say, 'The show also includes a brief venture into Grockery by its Simple Simon, Roy Castle, who in ten minutes of brilliantly gentle wordless fooling puts to shame all those joyless buffoons who misuse the great name of Clown in circus and theatre.' Hear, hear!

It was a very successful show backstage too. Alfred Marks and Paddy O'Neill were always ready to 'break me up' on stage, although this time any ad libbing that went on was shared with the audience. Sticking to the script had always been hard for me and the temptation is always there to come out with an extra bit of business, but I never do it with an actor who is easily thrown. That's my story anyway.

After our season at the Palladium, the following year we took the show to the Palace, Manchester, and it was there that I was involved in the greatest transformation scene ever witnessed.

Every weekend I travelled down to London by sleeper on Saturday night and flew back on the Monday morning plane. One unforgettable Monday, the plane was delayed – not enough to worry about at first, and Tommy Cooper, who was playing the Opera House, Manchester, was a most amiable companion at the bar. The delay continued until it was obviously going to be too late for me to get to the theatre in time for curtain-up. I rang the Palace and told them to put my understudy on. For some strange reason my stand-in was a diminutive lady of slight build who doubled as Mother

Goose, and could easily have fitted into the left leg of my costume. Anyway – on she went.

Meanwhile, back at Heathrow, Tommy Cooper was in the middle of performing his celebrated 'Eskimo taking a leak' impression using a handful of ice cubes as props, when our flight was suddenly called. I was met by a distraught manager at the airport and driven like the clappers to the theatre.

I arrived halfway through the first half, dressed in thirty seconds flat and got to the wings at the very moment that Betty Jumell, my understudy, was about to make her re-appearance on stage after being turned from a chicken into a human being – in the panto, that is. I thanked her hurriedly and ran on stage.

The gasp of astonishment from the kids which greeted my appearance was tremendous. The transformation was so great that there was a deathly hush for at least five minutes. And for pantomime that's a supreme achievement.

It wasn't so good for Tommy Cooper at the Opera House, though – his props had melted.

The next time I appeared at the Palladium, in 1961, Leslie McDonnell had taken over from Val Parnell as managing director. The show was called *Let Yourself Go* and I was re-united with my old mate Roy Castle in a cast that also included Marion Ryan, Audrey Jeans, Ronnie Corbett, The King Brothers and Eddie Calvert, the trumpet player who was then at the height of his career.

The sketches turned out to be less funny in practice than they looked on paper and we were taken to task for it by the critics. 'Mr Nesbitt's production has all the zip to which we have become accustomed over the years but *Let Yourself Go* is all zips and one begs to ask "Where are the trousers?" ' wrote Robert Muller in the *Daily Mail*. 'Harry Secombe ... wondrously has breath enough to exercise his tenor voice at the end, but except for a good moment as the fat woman of

the seaside postcards he is lost in tedious and banal sketches.'
That was what Michael Wall wrote in the *Guardian*, but he
had good things to say about Roy. 'Roy Castle is more
fortunate in having two long spots on his own and once again
shows he is a relaxed, talented and refreshingly unaffected
entertainer.' Roy was now well on his way to the top, but I was
not so sure about which way I was going.

There is one particular incident that makes this show
memorable for me.

The dress rehearsal had been something of a disaster in
which everything that could have gone wrong, did just that.
There's a saying in the profession that if the dress rehearsal
goes smoothly, the opening night will be a failure, so I
fervently hoped that the same would apply to our show.

Miraculously, the opening performance ran without any
hitches apart from a lack of laughter here and there and, after
the finale, I turned to Eddie Calvert, who was standing next to
me, and gave him a hug. 'We've done it Eddie,' I cried,
squeezing him hard in my relief.

'You've done my ribs in,' he gasped, clutching his chest.

Unfortunately, in my excitement that is exactly what I had
done. He had to be taken straight off to hospital where he was
strapped up.

It was a tribute to Eddie as an old trouper that he still
carried on with the show on the following day, although he
tackled the top notes on 'Oh my Papa' with a great deal of
caution.

In spite of the bad reviews, the show ran its allotted span
and the business was very good right up to the time we closed.
The sketches improved as the show progressed and Audrey
Jeans, with whom I had worked in pantomime, proved to be a
great help with the laughs. Ronnie Corbett was, as always,
worth his weight in gold and it was not long before his own
career took off.

*

The last revue that I was due to appear in at the 'Fab Pal' as Beryl Reid used to call it, was *London Laughs* which opened on 6 May 1966.

I had come back from America the previous November and was feeling pretty low after *Pickwick* had closed on Broadway. Then, after Christmas, Jimmy Grafton told me that Bernard Delfont wanted me to go back to the Palladium for the Summer Show. This bucked me up no end and I was looking forward to going to work again.

This time I had the support of Jimmy Tarbuck who had made a hit on *Sunday Night at the London Palladium*, Thora Hird and Freddie Frinton from TV's *Meet the Wife* series, the lovely Anita Harris, and another dear friend who had accompanied me on many overseas tours for the services, and Russ Conway who was billed as a special guest. Someone who was appearing for the first time at the theatre and worked with me in the sketches was Nicky Henson, the son of the great Leslie Henson, who has since turned out to be a very fine actor.

This time the show was almost universally panned. Barry Norman wrote, 'I could have almost wept, but I was too busy yawning.' Herbie Kretzmer wrote, 'It's all very glum and old-fashioned.' The *Punch* critic moaned, '*London Laughs* is a disgrace to the entertainment world.' Well, it wasn't quite *that* bad.

It was the year that the World Cup was hosted in England and business began to drop off quite alarmingly as most people were watching the football on the television.

One day Leslie McDonnell came into my room with a request. He wanted to take out the donkey and cart in which Thora and Freddie made their entrance in the first half finale. I didn't think it was a good idea to cut that particular bit, because it always got a good round of applause when the donkey came on. He accepted my decision gracefully and left.

A week later, when the business was still not picking up,

Leslie came in again, threw his hands up in despair and lamented 'That effing donkey is earning more money than I am.'

Being on stage with Jimmy Tarbuck was quite hazardous. I found him to be a really lovely guy and quite unselfish as a performer. But he would never keep still in the sketches, he was constantly on the move – so much so that one night I grabbed the back of his jacket to make him stand in position. When he went to move away, my grip on his jacket was so strong that I tore part of it off. To his credit he laughed, and the audience all thought it was part of the act. To me he is one of the funniest comics around and I like the way he has mellowed with age.

Hits and Mishaps
in Film and TV

After *London Laughs* I began to take more care with the material I had to work with. Too many times I had been presented with a *fait accompli* where the script was part and parcel of the deal, and I had accepted the fact. In reality, by this time television had made great inroads in theatre attendances and the big spectaculars were losing favour.

I had been involved in television very early on – in 1946, in fact, when I appeared in *Roof Top Rendezvous* after Cecil Madden had spotted me at the Windmill Theatre.

I did quite a bit of television work after that, mostly solo spots in Variety programmes, but also in a musical version of *Toad of Toad Hall* in which I played the Judge for two consecutive years. Then, when I appeared in summer season with Cyril Fletcher, I played in sketches in a television series with him.

For the life of me I cannot remember all the television programmes in which I was involved, but one stands out as a sort of watershed in my career on the box. It was a show from Radio Olympia in 1955 – broadcast live, as almost every programme was in those days. I was involved in all sorts of antics: marching with a Guards band, pretending to play a trombone with a busby down over my eyes – even riding a horse at one point in the proceedings. The whole show was performed in the vast arena at Olympia with the orchestra, conducted by Eric Robinson, situated on the far side of the hall.

The finale was my performance of 'Nessun Dorma', and because of the strict rules laid down by Ricordi's, the publishers of Puccini's music, the aria had to be sung in the costume of the opera. This posed several problems. I had to wear a Chinese tunic and a round pillbox hat and the time given for me to change was limited to the time it took for the George Mitchell Singers to sing the introductory bars to the aria. In addition, the pay-off to the sketch which immediately preceded the aria required me to be stranded half-way up a rope. During rehearsals I just about made it and the producer declared himself satisfied. I was a bit apprehensive, but being a dutiful sort of chap, I declared that I could manage the change in the allotted time.

Things did not work quite as planned for the actual recording. First of all, in the black-out which brought my sketch to an end, I was not lowered gently to the ground as rehearsed, but had to drop six feet to the floor of the arena, in darkness. Then, as I was frantically dressing into the Fu Manchu style outfit, I was told that six bars had been taken out of the introduction to save time. The result was that I stood in the arena, transfixed in the spotlight, half-buttoned into my costume, gasping for breath from the effort of falling from the rope.

As I began singing the opening bars I felt my chest heaving in panic, and when I came to the low notes my throat completely seized up. Eric Robinson – on the other side of the arena – was not fully aware of my plight and carried on with the music.

I had two options at this point – walk off in disgrace or explain my situation to the audience, the course of action I decided to take.

'Stop, Eric,' I cried, my voice rising a couple of octaves. 'I'm out of breath.'

Eric turned around in alarm and the whole orchestra came to a halt. Rosin filled the air over the string sections as their bows skidded across their instruments, a series of indelicate sounds came from the trombonists as they deflated their cheeks. The audience, meanwhile, went quiet with only a nervous titter here and there.

It was now up to me to explain what had happened – it was make or break time.

'I'm sorry,' I said, stepping forward. 'I've only had a few seconds to get ready and I lost my breath dropping from that flipping rope. Just give me a chance to get my breath back and I'll have another go.'

For a moment there was silence and I thought, 'That's it, Secombe, you've done it now.' Then there was a ripple of applause and some good-natured laughter and the moment passed.

'OK, Eric,' I called. 'I'm ready.'

The orchestra started from the beginning of the aria – without the Mitchell singers this time, and I launched myself into the aria. By some miracle I sang it as well as I had ever done and received a tremendous round of applause at the end.

After the show Ronnie Waldman, who was then Head of Television, came to see me. I thought he was going to tell me never to darken his screens again. But, instead, he stuck out his hand and said 'That was a real breakthrough, Harry. Now you are on your way.'

As a result of the Olympia show I was given a series by the BBC called *Secombe Here*, which was written by Jimmy Grafton and Eric Sykes. There was one particular programme which caused a bit of a stir even before it went out. In those days – the early 1950s – the BBC used to put on

Four original idiots.

Recording session with Marcel Stellman.

Peter making himself heard. (*Press Association*)

With a bewildered HRH at Peter's house in Elstead.

Busking for my TV show. We collected three quid. (*Daily Mirror*)

Last Goon Show of All – three Goons and a royal flush. (*BBC*)

Me, Spike and Eric as The Three Charlies – a strong-man act.

This Is Your Life in 1958. Peter and Spike duelling, with my parents in the background. (*BBC*)

Me as Pickwick in 1963. The hat hides a bald wig. (*Daily Mirror*)

Secombe on Broadway, folks! (*Daily Mail*)

Making-up for *The Four Musketeers* in my dressing room at Drury Lane. David is holding Katy who isn't too impressed.

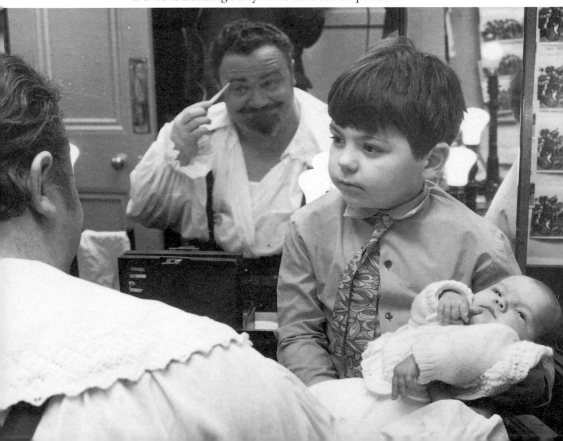

On set for *Song Of Norway*, with my idol Edward G Robinson and Liz Larner.

Myself as Schippel in *The Plumber's Progress*. Roger Kemp watching me go a funny colour as I hit a high note. (*Tom Hustler*)

With Hattie Jacques, Jimmy Edwards and Eric Sykes in the bushes in a scene from *Rhubarb*. The dialogue was easy as 'rhubarb' was all anybody said.

At a Royal Command Performance with Eartha Kitt. Cliff Richard looks
a little apprehensive to my left.

With HRH at an Army benevolent fund concert. Jennifer is enjoying
herself. (*Press Association*)

The lovely Adele Leigh and me on the set of *Davy*. (*Ealing Films*)

Oliver asking for 'more' from Peggy Mount and me. He'll be lucky.

'Interludes' in the periods between transmissions. One Interlude was a short film of a potter at his wheel, another was of a leisurely trip down the Thames in the Maidenhead area, and in order to publicize my show we filmed a couple of parodies of these Interludes, recorded in exactly the same venues, to go out as trailers.

In the potter's wheel film, everything was as per the genuine one, until the clay on the wheel began to wobble all over the place and the camera panned up from the ads to reveal an idiotically grinning Secombe.

For the Thames one, we pin-pointed the very bend of the river near Medmenham, from which the original film started and, as in the genuine film, our camera drifted down the river, in a scene of riparian tranquillity, until suddenly I popped up out of the water with a notice saying 'Don't forget to watch *Secombe Here* tonight'. Of course, this meant that I had to go, fully dressed, over the side of the boat carrying the camera crew, submerge and appear with the notice held above my head.

The current was pretty strong that day and the clothes I was wearing dragged me down after the boat went past. Everybody on board was laughing and congratulating each other on getting the shot at the first attempt, while I was getting more waterlogged by the minute. It was only when one of the boat's crew realized that I really was in difficulty that I was pulled out of the water. By that time I was beginning to think that there must be an easier way to make a living.

Another gimmick we used to publicize the show was for me to be seen for a fleeting moment on other people's programmes. During the opening sequence of the popular panel show *What's My Line?*, as the camera moved along the faces of the panel, I was revealed with my usual stupid smile. I also turned up on other shows as a member of the studio audience. It was all great fun and everyone concerned entered into the spirit of the occasion, and apparently these ground-breaking ideas seemed to work because we had a huge viewing audience when the programmes went out.

The show itself had a surprise ending too. Eric Sykes had the brilliant idea of having a big fencing finale at the closing credits. Some of the audience had been provided with prop swords and as we came to the end of the programme, Eric, Spike Milligan and I fought our way off stage, past the cameras and up through the audience into the street outside the Shepherds Bush Empire where the show was being televised – live, of course. We got into a waiting open-topped car and waved our swords as the credits rolled over our retreating figures.

It was the custom in those days for the evening news to be read over a static shot of Big Ben with the hands at 10 o'clock. When the news finished there was a live studio shot of Peter Haig reading the weather forecast and wishing everybody 'Good night'.

Bill Lyon-Shaw, the producer of *Secombe Here*, arranged for Eric, Spike and me to burst into Peter Haig's little studio, still brandishing our swords. Peter then moved across to the Big Ben mock-up, removed one of the hands and joined in the fight. After we had been ejected from his studio, Peter calmly combed back his hair, apologized and bade the viewers his customary farewell.

This was the first time that the BBC had agreed to let its hair down on television, and the public reaction to all the shenanigans was most favourable.

The *Secombe Here* shows also saw me singing quite a bit of opera, although whenever a guest opera star joined me in a duet, special permission had to be obtained from whatever opera company the artist was under contract to. My reputation for fooling around was well known and I had to promise faithfully that I would behave.

It was decided that I would do the love duet from *Madam*

Butterfly with the lovely soprano Adele Leigh. This was the first time we had worked together, and she was naturally somewhat nervous at our first rehearsal with Eric Robinson and the orchestra, but she seemed satisfied that I would be able to cope with the music. Once again, the copyrigh for the duet was held by Ricordi, and it had to be performed in the appropriate costume. As Lieutenant Pinkerton, this meant that I had to be dressed in the white tropical uniform of an American naval officer, and Adele was to wear the traditional garb of a geisha girl, complete with black wig, wooden shoes and floor-length kimono.

At the final run-through for the cameras, neither of us was in complete costume, we just went through the duet on the set. It was a pretty setting, based on the Willow Pattern plates, with a little ornamental bridge over which I was to make my entrance. Overhanging the bridge was a fake willow tree and there were two steps at the other end of it down which I was to join Adele for the main part of the duet. Everything seemed to go well, even though I was a bit embarrassed at having to clutch Adele to my chest at the climax, but she didn't seem to mind.

My uniform was ready in time for the show, which again was a live broadcast, and it was not quite as dashing as I had hoped. I was about seventeen stone in those days and the jacket revealed more of my paunch than I would have liked. The epaulets had been sewn on to the shoulders, but didn't look too safe to me. The trousers were not too bad, but I would never have been able to sit down in them. The hat, although realistic, came down low over my ears when I put it on my head. 'Keep your head back a bit,' said the floor manager, responding to a call in his ear-piece from the control gallery. 'You'll throw a shadow over your face if you don't.'

I nodded nervously and the cap came down again. 'See what I mean?' he hissed, as we stood waiting for the introduction to start the duet.

My cue came up and I started across the bridge. Unfortunately a twig from the over-hanging willow tree caught under my right epaulet, causing it to become detached from my shoulder, and it hung down like the red tabs on a general's lapel. My hat slipped forward in the process and I stood on the end of the bridge almost blinded as I sang, in Italian, 'Let me kiss your dear hand.'

Adele, who had never seen me in my costume, didn't know whether to laugh or cry when she caught sight of the man she, as Butterfly, would commit suicide over. Instead, she gave a stifled snort as I advanced down the steps toward her.

I was now at her side, looking straight up her nose. The added height of her wooden shoes and the geisha wig meant that she towered over me. The peak of my cap was jutting into her chest, so I did the only thing in the circumstances – hurled it to the ground. It should be remembered, that while all this was going on we were singing a passionate love duet.

Adele bent her knees under her kimono to accommodate my lack of stature, which was fine until just before the end of the song she developed cramp and, as I sang the final bars, where I was supposed to clutch her to my chest, she suddenly straightened up and I found my nose pressed firmly in her bosom.

It is a great tribute to Adele as a performer and as a person that we managed to finish our duet without her losing any of her dignity.

Mine, of course, was in tatters.

For some years I did an hour-long Saturday evening show for BBC Television entitled *Secombe and Friends*. It consisted of sketches written by Jimmy Grafton along with Peter Vincent and David Nobbs, and was directed by Terry Hughes.

One of my most enchanting guests was a young New Zealand soprano who had only recently arrived to sing at Covent Garden. At rehearsals I had difficulty in pronouncing her name properly. After a few attempts at it, she laughed and said, 'Just call me Tin Knickers.'

That was my first introduction to Kiri te Kanawa. She was a delight to work with and was very patient with me as I wrestled with the tenor part of a duet from Bizet's *Carmen*. We were all very impressed by this lovely lady from the Antipodes and it was obvious that she was going to be a big star in the operatic firmament.

Another great lady with whom I had the pleasure of performing was Eartha Kitt. The first time we met was at the flat she was renting in London, where we were due to go through the script and discuss the routine of a duet we were going to perform together on the show.

I was driving up from Swansea for the meeting and on the way I was caught up in a horrendous traffic jam. The result was that I was over an hour late arriving, something I always dread because I am very particular about punctuality.

I had heard tales of Eartha's fiery temper, and it was with fear and trembling that I knocked on the front door of her mews flat. When the door was opened, the scowl on her face as she greeted me seemed to confirm my worst suspicions. I began to stammer my apologies which she listened to in stony silence. Then, suddenly, she threw her head back and laughed. 'It's all right, man, come in and have a coffee.' She had just been putting on an act – and from then on it was laughter all the way.

The duet we performed was 'Sweethearts' from the operetta *Rose Marie*, which was made famous by Jeanette McDonald and Nelson Eddy. I had queried the choice of music with Jimmy Grafton. 'She'll never get those top notes,' I said. 'Her voice is too low.'

'You'll be surprised,' said Jimmy. And I was. In addition to the well-known 'purring' sound she produced in songs like 'I'm Just An Old Fashioned Girl', she also possessed a lovely, clear top register, which completely bowled me over.

In the actual sketch she lay centre-stage on a *chaise-longue* in a sequinned gown with a feather in a bandeau around her head à la Red Indian squaw. When the music began I sang the opening line off stage.

'When I'm calling you-oo-oo-oo-oo-ooh,' I yodelled as I stood in the wings dressed in a travesty of a Royal Canadian mounted policeman's uniform, with breeches which spread out from my hips and finished about six inches above my ankles, and a hat several sizes too big.

'And I answer too-oo-oo-oo-oo-oo,' carolled Eartha in her sweet soprano.

Then I made my entrance. Eartha had not seen me in costume at the rehearsal, and she nearly choked with laughter at my comical appearance. The scene was a riot in the studio and was such a success that we repeated it later that year for a Royal Command Performance.

Eartha really was a pleasure to work with and we became great chums. The last time I met her, she flung her arms around my neck and there were genuine tears in her eyes.

One of my most memorable early television appearances was when I was involved in the first ever live link between London and New Zealand. I was in New Zealand doing a series of concerts, and the BBC thought it would be a great idea for me to appear live from Auckland on a *Cilla Black Show*.

Owing to the time difference between the two countries, I had to get up very early, and much was made of this for the broadcast. A bed was placed on the top of a hill outside Auckland, and I had to pretend to wake up, chat with Cilla and then sing a song which had been pre-recorded.

At that time there was only one colour television camera in the whole of New Zealand and everyone was keeping their fingers crossed that the enterprise would work. A van containing the sound equipment was driven up on to the hill so that I could hear my music through the speakers that were strategically placed around the area. There was also going to be a time lag between Cilla's questions to me and my answers, and vice versa, so the idea was for each to wait for the other to stop talking before answering, otherwise there would be an overlap.

Everything was set up beautifully and the picture was looking good on the monitor when, with only seconds to go, the sound system refused to work. The director wrenched out the ear-piece he was using to communicate with London and bunged it in my ear. The result was that I had to chat with Cilla and sing my song with only the comparatively faint sound from the ear-piece to guide me. Cilla and I overlapped so badly that it was decided that I ought to get into the song as soon as possible. Because the wire attached to the thing in my ear was not very long, my movements as I sang were severely restricted and I must have looked a proper twit standing on top of a hill in New Zealand wearing a night gown and night cap singing the theme song from *The Onedin Line* at least a bar out of synch.

However, everyone seemed to love the fact that they were watching me being an idiot on live television all the way from the southern hemisphere, and we got a cable later that morning from the BBC engineers saying that we had made history.

To be Welsh and in show business is to belong to a rather exclusive club. We all know each other – indeed we seek each other out – and when we get together we become even more Welsh than ever. Our veneer of sophistication is only finger-nail deep in most cases and we flaunt our working-class backgrounds like battle flags.

Stanley Baker and I were great mates and another good friend was Donald Houston, with whom I first worked in a radio play called *This Vale of Tears* by Cliff Gordon. Geraint

Evans and I performed together several times and the harpist Ossian Ellis was a frequent member of the *Goon Show* orchestra.

It just so happened that one year the five of us were recording a Christmas television show from the ABC studios at Elstree and, in between takes, we got chatting about Richard Burton and his affair with Elizabeth Taylor. What incensed us was the cavalier way that Richard was treating his wife, Sybil, a Welsh girl we all knew. It was the time when the affair was at its height, and Stanley knew that Richard and Elizabeth were filming at the MGM studios in nearby Borehamwood.

The recording took quite some time and in the intervals we availed ourselves of the generous hospitality of the ABC management. As the hours went by, we got more and more 'tanked up' and our determination to tell Richard exactly what we thought of him for what he was doing to Sybil grew to such an extent that Stanley made a phone call to the MGM studios. He discovered that Richard and Elizabeth would be in the pub next door and that the media were not around.

It was decided that we would drive there as soon as our recording was finished and have it out with our recalcitrant fellow Welshman. Recording over, we piled out to the car park. I had a Thunderbird in those days which only took two passengers, but somehow five of us managed to fit in.

Together we stood uncertainly outside the pub and then we burst in. There was no one in the bar except, at the end of the room, Richard Burton and Elizabeth Taylor, who was drinking a pint of beer.

'This is it,' said Stanley, who was the bravest of us, and began to move forward.

Richard watched him coming and suddenly burst into song with the opening lines, in Welsh, of 'Counting the Goats'.

We all stopped in our tracks and joined in with him. Two hours later, after we had sung ourselves hoarse and Burton had silenced Elizabeth's attempt to join in with 'Sing your own bloody songs,' the party broke up amid back slappings and mutual expressions of good will.

Outside again, I turned to Stanley and said, 'We never did mention Sybil, boyo.'

'We didn't, did we? Bloody shame,' said Stanley. And that was that.

When I got home I said to Myra, 'You're much better looking than Elizabeth Taylor.'

She sniffed. 'Now I know you're drunk,' she said.

The author and director Noel Langley approached me in 1954 and asked me to play Barizel, the leader of the students, in a film called *Svengali*. It was a much larger production than any of the previous ones in which I had appeared, and was to star Hildegard Neff and Robert Newton as Trilby and Svengali. It also featured a number of the Rank Charm School graduates – Terence Morgan, Derek Bond and Hubert Gregg, for example. Paul Rogers and Noel Purcell were also in the cast, and Alfie Bass and I were supplying the comedy element.

Noel Langley was an aficionado of the *Goon Show* and had laughed so much at our antics when lying in a hospital bed recovering from an eye operation, that the tears had run down his cheeks and greatly assisted his recovery. He thought that a bit of lunacy from me would help to give the plot a much needed lift.

The story concerned an artist's model, Trilby – supposedly Irish, but Ms Neff's German accent somewhat strained the credulity of the audience – who meets up with three students, Billy, Taffy and the Laird, in Paris. She also makes the acquaintance of the sinister Svengali. Billy and Trilby fall in love and Svengali becomes wildly jealous. Billy's parents also hate the match and try to make Trilby leave Paris. Svengali takes delight in taunting Billy over this. Billy attacks Svengali and is subsequently trampled by bolting horses and badly injured (making Terence Morgan's portrayal of Billy even more intriguing by having to cope with a limp). Exciting stuff, eh?

Meanwhile, Trilby falls under Svengali's hypnotic powers, becoming a great singer under his influence and forgetting her former life. When Billy attempts to visit her at a concert in Covent Garden, Svengali has him thrown out. Svengali then declares his love for his protégée and tells her that if she dies, so will he. At the opening of the concert he becomes ill and his powers over Trilby fail – and she can no longer sing (Hildegard Neff couldn't anyway, her voice was dubbed). The audience give her the bird, she lapses into a coma (sensible girl) and we assume that Svengali's prophecy will come true. However, limping little Billy brings her back to life and the spell is broken. End of story.

Somewhere in all of this Trilby poses nude in the studio run by Carrel, played by Alfie Bass, and I ran amok as the leader of the art students, mugging disgracefully in the process.

The first days of filming at Shepperton Studios were fine. Robert Newton, a notorious drinker, had promised Noel Langley and George Minter, the producer, that he would go on the wagon until the film was finished. I found him a charming man and he told me lots of stories about the films he had appeared in – *Treasure Island, The Citadel*, etc. – he was great to work with and it was a wonderful experience for me to see screen acting by a master of the genre at first hand.

But I came to work one morning to find that pandemonium had broken out. Newton had arrived at the studios smashed out of his mind and proceeded to drop his trousers in front of the make-up ladies. He then chased the lighting cameraman around the studio with a knife swearing 'I'll teach you to paint your effing pictures in lights.'

He was removed from the set and dropped from the picture. The next we heard was that he had flown off to California. I don't think he ever returned to England after that. It was a pity because he had such a towering talent when he was sober.

Newton's replacement was Donald Wolfit, who gave an entirely different slant on the character of Svengali. I'm afraid that in one scene with him, Alfie Bass and I had the giggles so badly that Noel Langley banned us from the set until we had pulled ourselves together. However in *The Film Bulletin* Wolfit is described as giving 'a performance of uninhibited bravura with moments even, of grandeur'. Ms Neff's Trilby was called 'handsome but spiritless'. In other words, as someone unkindly said, 'A naff Neff performance'.

Mercifully I was not singled out for criticism, apart from being described in the 12 January 1955 edition of *Variety* as part of 'a safe supporting cast'.

One who was well down on the list of supporting players was a young actor fresh from RADA. He had won the Gold Medal for his acting that year and had been given one line in the film as part of his award. All he had to say in a scene with me and Alfie Bass was 'Have you heard that Van Gogh has cut off his ear at Arles?' Not much of a début on the silver screen, but it got Jeremy Brett off on a soaring career. All it got from our two characters after the director said 'Cut' were two resounding raspberries.

It was through my friendship with Stanley Baker that I met the American producer Cy Enfield at a party at Stanley and his wife Ellen's house in Wimbledon. Cy was one of the unfortunate members of the film industry who had been hounded out of Hollywood by the McCarthy witch-hunt.

Fortunately for me, at this time – in 1959 – he was preparing a new production to be filmed at Pinewood Studios. It was to be called *Jet Stream*, but the name was later changed to *Jet Storm* for some obscure reason. Cy thought that I would be just right for the part of Binky Meadows, a vaudeville star who was one of the passengers on a plane heading for New York from London Airport.

In the story, one of the passengers, scientist Ernest Tilley (played by Richard Attenborough), accuses another passenger, James Brock (George Rose), of being the hit-and-run driver who had killed his child. The captain, played by Stanley Baker, questions Tilley and finds that he has planted a bomb on the plane. The other passengers led by an industrialist called Mulliner (Patrick Allen) are stopped by the captain from finding out where the bomb is and so they plot to murder Brock in the hope of appeasing Tilley. Not good old Binky, though. I never left my seat for one minute. Brock, however, brings about his own death in a moment of panic – Hooray! Eventually a small boy is persuaded to appeal to Tilley, who defuses the bomb and the plane touches down safely.

Nearly all my scenes were shot sitting next to dear Dame Sybil Thorndike, another passenger, who was an excellent companion to have and subsequently became a good friend. She was a remarkable lady who never fluffed a line or complained about anything. I learned a lot from her.

The only thing that worried me about the film when we were shooting was that the clouds which appeared outside the windows of the plane never moved. 'Don't worry,' said Dame Syb. 'They'll think of something.' But they didn't – and if you ever see the film on television – about three o'clock in the morning as a rule – you'll see what I mean.

The reviews of *Jet Storm* were not too bad. *Variety* said 'A workmanlike suspense drama with some excellent acting cameos by an all-star cast. Stand out comedy relief is provided by Harry Secombe and Sybil Thorndyke, a most unlikely combination which nevertheless combines like bacon and eggs.'

I'm rather proud of that.

Davy was to be my big chance to score a success in films, something I had longed to do ever since I started in the business. My previous attempts at becoming a film star were pretty poor to put it mildly.

Penny Points to Paradise, made in Brighton with Alfred Marks and Bill Kerr, was great fun to do but hardly advaned any of our careers. *Down Among the Z Men*, an E J Fancy production, featured all the Goons plus Carole Carr and Andrew Timothy, the TV Toppers and a number of small-part players. That too was something of a disaster, emerging every so often through the years on late night or early morning television, forever consigned to that Sargasso Sea of the cinema. *Forces Sweetheart* with Michael Bentine, Freddy Finton, Hy Hazell and myself also failed to impress either the public or the critics. If you happen to come across the title in any of the books which list movies on television, you won't find any stars alongside it. Exclamation marks, certainly.

And so, when Michael Balcon decided to star me in one of his films made in co-operation with MGM at Elstree Studios I was over the moon with excitement.

William Rose, the American writer who was responsible for *Genevieve* and the prestigious *Guess Who's Coming to Dinner?* was signed up to write the script, Basil Dearden was to produce and Michael Relph was to direct. Normally they worked the other way around, with Basil directing and Michael producing. Geoffrey Unsworth was the camera man with a host of credits to his name.

Bill Rose came up to Coventry, where I was playing at the New Theatre, to chat with me about the script. He was an extremely nice man and we got on very well together. The idea he had for the story was one which appealed to me. It was about a young comic called Davy, the mainstay of a family act working in Variety who, because of his tenor voice, had been granted an audition with a famous conductor at Covent Garden. The audition was held on stage at the Opera House but things went wrong when his young nephew, who had come along with Davy, knocked over some scenery backstage just as he was finishing his aria. Without waiting to hear what the conductor had to say about him, Davy grabbed the lad and ran out of the theatre.

However, the great conductor was so impressed by Davy's voice that he tracked him down at the Music Hall where he was performing at and offered him a career in opera.

In the end, Davy, faced with the dilemma of furthering his singing career at the expense of the family act, decides to stay with the act – at the same time turning down the prospect of a romance with a soprano (played by Adele Leigh) he had met in the canteen at Covent Garden.

That, roughly, was the story, but there was an added complication. Bill decided that the action should take place during the actual time the film took to run. In other words, the ninety minutes or so on the screen would be the timescale of the action, thus preserving the continuity of time. This meant that there were to be no flashbacks – all the history of Davy's family act and the undercurrents of past conflict had to be revealed in the dialogue.

Another added dimension was the fact that it was to be shot in Technirama, a new wide-screen process.

The cast list included Ron Randell, Susan Shaw, Bill Owen, Peter Frampton, George Relph, Alexander Knox, Gladys Henson and Joan Sims.

The first week of shooting meant that I had to be on set early every morning, working until late in the evening and so arrangements were made for me to stay at the Edgewarebury Country Club near the studios.

It was my first real experience of what it meant to be a star working in a major studio. Every possible comfort was provided for me – a canvas chair with my name emblazoned on the back, a dressing-room, filled with fruit and flowers, which had only recently been vacated by Van Johnson was mine for the run of the film, and any time I worked up a sweat there was a make-up girl to pat my face with a soft leather cloth soaked in eau-de-cologne. During breaks on the set, tea and sandwiches were brought to me by my stand-in, who also took the brunt of the standing around for the lighting cameraman.

Penny Points to Paradise was nothing to all this, I thought to myself.

When I got home to Cheam on the Friday night of that first week, I sat in my armchair by the fire in the front room. It was a pretty wild night outside which made me appreciate even more the warmth inside, and as I looked into the dying embers in the grate my mind went over the events of the past five days. 'I'm a star,' I thought. 'A proper film star at last. Pampered on the set, provided with every possible comfort off it – this is the life for me.' I crossed my legs and leant my head back against the chair, smiling with self-satisfaction.

My reverie was interrupted by Myra coming in from the kitchen. She had a very heavy cold, her hair was windswept and she had a bucket in her hand. She looked at me for a moment, taking in my relaxed attitude.

'Come on, Gregory Peck,' she said, 'get some bloody coal on the fire!'

Ah well.

The audition scene in *Davy* really worried me because it was going to be filmed on location on stage at the Covent Garden Opera House. I had already recorded 'Nessun Dorma', the audition piece, with the full orchestra and everyone assured me that I had done a good job on it. However, I knew that I would be coming under the scrutiny of real opera singers who would have every reason to regard me as an upstart with no operatic pedigree. So it was with much trepidation that I waited in the stalls while the preliminary shots were taken of the stage, which was packed with the actual members of the current production, *Die Meistersingers*, being cleared for my audition piece. I saw Joan Sutherland and Hans Hoffer, a fine Wagnerian tenor, being ushered into the wings, and my heart thumped.

After what seemed an eternity, I heard my name being called by the assistant director and I weaved my way through the stalls to where I was to make my entrance. The opera chorus had now taken to sitting up in the circle to watch the proceedings and had not, as I had hoped, gone off to their dressing-rooms or the canteen, or anywhere where I could be seen and heard.

Alexander Knox, as the conductor, motioned me to the front of the stage, where I announced what I was going to sing. The actual recording had begun with just piano and then with typical artistic licence the full sound of the orchestra crept in after a few bars.

I was petrified, which was what I was supposed to be in the film, but I was determined to break the ice somehow. So I retreated upstage, and as the piano track started I came forward, opened my mouth and sang 'I've got a lovely bunch of coconuts'. Fortunately, everybody laughed, and the dreadful moment was over.

It's something I have always done, I suppose, to pre-empt criticism – like blowing a raspberry after telling a joke. Sometimes it works and sometimes it doesn't, but on that occasion it certainly did.

By contrast with the Covent Garden scenes, those of the Music Hall theatre were shot on location at Collins Music Hall, where the dampness in the dressing-rooms was so evident, that the walls ran with water. It seemed a waste to me to use a new colour technique on such drabness, though it came in to good effect in a slap-stick routine in which lots of different coloured paint was sloshed about in the family act. Charlie Cairoli, the great clown who was such a feature at Blackpool's Tower Circus, came down at my request to stage the scene and a good job he did of it, too.

Davy premièred at the Empire, Leicester Square on the same night that Peter Sellers's film *Nothing But the Truth*, opened at the Odeon. Spike Milligan declared that he was going to set up a magic lantern in the middle of the square and have his own première, but I don't think anything came of it.

The critics didn't take kindly to *Davy*. Donald Zec in the *Daily Mirror* said of me 'He sings like Caruso – Sugar Ray Robinson Caruso.'

I think part of the reason why *Davy* failed to impress was the fact that it was billed as a 'zany' type movie, over-emphasizing the comedy content, whereas it was mostly a dramatic story. Anyway it was not the stepping stone to stardom that I had hoped it would be.

It was many years before I made another film.

When Jimmy Grafton told me that Richard Lester wanted me to play the role of the Shelter Man in his feature film of *The Bed-Sitting Room*, I was intrigued, to say the least. I had seen the original play by Spike Milligan and John Antrobus and had enjoyed it, but I didn't see how it could be made into a film because the plot was so bizarre.

It was about a group of survivors living a precarious existence three years after a nuclear war had devastated the world. Among them are Captain Bules Martin and Lord Fortnum who is terrified of turning into a bed-sitting room. The survivors are joined by Penelope, her lover, Alan, Father and Mother who have been living on the Circle Line tube. Prior to the holocaust, the Shelter Man had been the Head of a regional seat of government, and the whole society is watched over by two policemen, played by Dudley Moore and Peter Cook, suspended in a balloon.

Eventually, Mother changes into a cupboard, Penny marries Bules Martin and Father is selected as Prime Minister, but is changed into a parakeet and subsequently eaten. Penelope ends her eighteen-month pregnancy by giving birth to a monster and Fortnum becomes the bed-sitting room. The country is eventually saved and Ethel Shroake rules over it as monarch. How's that for a plot!

When Richard Lester's offer came through I was starring in *The Four Musketeers* at Drury Lane and welcomed the opportunity to try something different – the constant repetition of a long run was getting to me.

The cast list for *The Bed-Sitting Room* made remarkable reading – Ralph Richardson, Michael Hordern, Arthur Lowe, Rita Tushingham, Spike Milligan, Mona Washbourne, Marty Feldman, Jimmy Edwards, as well as Peter Cook and Dudley Moore. Who could resist joining a cast of that magnitude? Unfortunately, the nature of the scenes in which I appeared meant that I only met up with two of those illustrious names.

My scenes in the studio were confined to the inside of a corrugated iron underground shelter littered with debris. Mona Washbourne as Mother was called upon to throw crockery at me when, in my role as the Shelter Man, I requested her to remind me of the wife I had lost. Mona threw the pots with such enthusiasm that the poor lady broke her ankle on the china-strewn floor of the shelter. However, like the trouper she was, she carried on with her ankle in plaster.

The rest of my participation in the film was shot on a rubbish dump somewhere off the North Circular, in the company of Michael Hordern, a most pleasant man to be with at any time. We were positioned at perilous positions among the garbage so that as he poured me a cup of tea the liquid appeared to be leaving the spout at an unusual angle – demonstrating the effect of the nuclear holocaust on the force of gravity. I must say that I quite enjoyed my couple of days on the rubbish tip with Richard Lester and Michael Hordern, though I certainly appreciated my comfortable, warm dressing-room at Drury Lane when I returned to it in the evening.

The critics did not much like the film when it was released, complaining about the lack of story line. However, there was one cinema in Sydney which ran *The Bed-Sitting Room* for several months. I happened to be playing at a theatre in the city at the time and the cinema manager invited me to make an appearance on stage between showings of the film. When I did so I was surprised at the reception I received. Later though, after thanking me for coming, the manager said 'It beats me, mate. I can't understand what the fuss is all about.'

One afternoon as I was settling down for a nap on the front patio of our house in Majorca, I heard someone walking up the steps. To my surprise it was Eric Sykes. He had come to ask me if I would like to play a golf-mad vicar in a short film he had written, and rather than send the script by post, he decided to outline the plot to me in person.

The plot concerned a police inspector and a vicar who were very competitive golfers, and the film followed them around the course as they both employed every trick in the book to win the match. In the end the vicar overdoes it by invoking the Almighty to help him once too often and is struck by a bolt of lightning. The vicar is reduced to the remains of two smoking shoes in the sand of a bunker.

The script was very easy to learn because it consisted of just one word – 'Rhubarb'.

It was great fun to make and Eric had dreamed up some unusual methods of cheating at golf. At one point I appear to be walking across the surface of a small lake, pulling my trolley along behind me. This effect was achieved by laying planks just below the surface of the lake along which I had to stride without looking down. I confess that I got very wet before I finally achieved the result that Eric desired.

I understand that *Rhubarb* is still a favourite at various golf clubs for screening on the odd social occasions.

It was while I was performing at the London Palladium in 1966 that Lewis Gilbert invited me to read for the part of Mr Bumble, the Beadle in the musical film version of *Oliver!* I was subsequently signed up – the first member of the cast to be contracted for the film, even before Ron Moody who had been such a wonderful Fagin in the stage production. Not a lot of people know that.

For some reason, Lewis Gilbert was replaced as director of the film by Sir Carol Reed before filming began, but luckily my contract was secure.

It was apparent from the very first day on the set at Shepperton Studios that we were working on a winner. The money being spent on the project was tangible. To wander round the outdoor sets was to be taken back in time. No wonder John Box was nominated for an Oscar for best set design, his recreation of early Victorian London was authentic down to the tiniest detail. There were even real loaves of bread in the baker's shop windows.

Carol Reed was a film actor's dream director. He never raised his voice in anger and before shooting every morning he would sit down with the cast members involved in the forthcoming scene and go over the action. He would remind us of the scene which preceded the one we were about to enact – the previous scene may have been filmed over a week before – so that we all had the right motivation and emotions in mind.

His only notes to me concerned my eyebrows. He warned me to stop moving them up and down to emphasize each point. 'On that big screen,' he explained, 'it will look as if your eyebrows are jumping six feet at a time!'

The first scenes to be filmed were the ones set in the workhouse where Mark Lester, as Oliver, is prodded by the other boys into asking for more gruel. The famous request for more was followed by a frantic chase around the dining tables in which Peggy Mount and I took part. When Oliver is eventually caught, Bumble, my character, had to seize the wriggling Oliver by his ear and march him off between the tables to be chastised by the Governors, all the while singing 'Oliver, Oliver, never before has a boy wanted more . . . etc.'

This was my very first appearance on set and, knowing my own strength, I was very wary that I might hurt the fragile Mark. At the first rehearsal I pulled his ear rather gingerly.

'No, no, Harry,' said Carol. 'You must really seize hold of his ear as roughly as you can.'

'He's such a delicate little lad,' I replied. (Incidentally, he is now about six foot three.)

'Never mind that,' said this previously compassionate director. 'Do it harder next time.'

We waited until the cameras and lights were ready for another take, and off we went again. When we got to the same piece of action, I really put everything I had into grabbing Mark's ear. To my horror it came away in my hand. The props man had fitted a false plastic ear on the boy. I had been set up rather beautifully, but I had to sit down for a while before I was ready for another take.

Peggy Mount, who was playing Mrs Bumble, was a joy to work with. She was the exact opposite of the dragon-like roles she often portrayed on stage and screen. I first met her at the Anvil Studios in Denham where the music for *Oliver!* was recorded, and I was a little in awe of her because of her screen reputation. However, she turned out to be a sweet, gentle soul who was apprehensive about having to sing with me.

The orchestra was under the direction of John Green, a famous Hollywood conductor with perfect pitch, an accomplishment which he was determined to demonstrate at every opportunity. He could pick out a bum note almost before it was played, and would bawl out the offending musician in front of the whole orchestra.

As we stood together watching the run-through of our music, Peggy and I looked at each other in alarm. Even though I had thoroughly rehearsed the number with the rehearsal pianist I was still likely to go off key with the full orchestra, until I had become accustomed to the orchestrations. In addition, the instruments being played were the ones in use at the time of the young Queen Victoria – crum horns, serpents and the like – and not very easy to follow.

It was going to be a bit of an ordeal for me, but for poor Peggy, who was not a singer, it was going to be a nightmare. I made a couple of tentative jokes in an attempt to get a laugh out of the musicians in the orchestra – some of whom I had worked with before. They got a bit of a titter, but not from John Green – who didn't know me from Adam – and was anxious to get on with the recording.

It was my turn to sing first and after a couple of mistakes I managed to get through the rehearsal without too much trouble. Peggy, though, was completely at sea and had great difficulty in picking up her opening note. John Green didn't do much to settle her down and in his exasperation became somewhat sarcastic, which resulted in Peggy shedding a few tears.

Eventually we both got it right and the sound recordist pronounced his satisfaction, but it was an unsettling couple of hours for everybody except Green.

When we were filming the 'Boy for sale' scene, I had to trudge through the fake snow hand-in-hand with Mark Lester, miming to the words of the song. Now, to get the effect of a heavy snowfall, a large fan blew pieces of jabolite, a sort of polystyrene, into our faces as we walked through the outside set. It looked great on the screen, but it was awkward for me to pretend to sing because the 'snow' was stinging my face. After a few takes I started to get the hang of it and Carol Reed told me to open my mouth wide for the long note at the end of the song. This had to be held for about fifteen seconds, and I was doing fine until a particularly large chunk of jabolite went straight down my throat, nearly choking me. Everybody had a good laugh – and so did I once I had managed to cough up the offending object. Once again I had the feeling that I had been set up.

Oliver! was great fun to do and I learned a great deal from being directed by Carol Reed.

My next appearance on film was as Bjornsterne Bjornson in *Song of Norway* and came as the result of the husband and wife, producer/director team of Andrew and Virginia Stone having seen my performance in *Oliver!* They decided that I was just the man they wanted to play the part of the famous Norwegian playwright, Bjornson. They contacted my agent and he set up a meeting in my St James's Place office for them to run over the music for me. They brought with them the film's songwriters, Robert Wright and George Forrest, to play their tunes on my piano.

It was reminiscent of an old Hollywood 'B' feature. Bob and George sat side by side on a small stool playing the music together on my small upright piano, while Andrew Stone, a grizzled veteran of God knows how many films – including W C Fields's final one – shouted out the plot.

'See now, this is when the kid comes into the piano store run by Eddie Robinson an' wants to buy a pianner for Grieg, see.'

'You mean Edward G Robinson?' I had to interrupt. I had seen every gangster film Edward G had ever made and, like many other budding comedians, I used to do an impression of him. If *he* was in the film, *I* had to be in it too.

Andrew Stone was a bit miffed at having his 'spiel' interrupted. 'Yeah, he's in it,' he said and went on with his summary of the plot.

I didn't need to hear any more. I was hooked, but allowed a decent time to elapse – during which Andrew described the complicated lifestory of Grieg (to be played by Toralv Maurstad, of whom I had *not* heard) – before my hand shot up and I agreed to take on the part.

Filming began for me in Lillehammer, Norway after I had enjoyed a break in the sun of Barbados with Myra and our youngest child, Katy.

The difference in climate was extreme. I left the 80 degrees of the West Indies for the minus 30 degrees of the frozen north. It was so cold on location that the hairs in my nostrils froze and ice would form in the corners of my eyes. Moving my lips to speak the dialogue was a distinct effort, resulting in one disastrous episode when I was required to drive an old-fashioned sleigh. Seated beside me was Elizabeth Larner, who was playing Bjornson's wife, and in the two seats behind us, Mr and Mrs Grieg – Toralv Marstad and Florence Henderson.

My single previous experience of driving horses had been in Llangyfelach, holding the reins of my uncle's old mare as we rode round the country lanes delivering blocks of fuel. There was nothing to it – the horse knew all the stops anyway and the only time she broke into a trot was when she could smell the home stables.

Lillehammer was quite a different kettle of fish to Llangyfelach. I found myself in charge of two fjord horses who had never worked as a pair before, and faced with the formidable task of following a complicated track which included a sharp right hand bend at the bottom of a steep hill. All this was undertaken in a temperature well below freezing and with a covering of nine inches of snow on the ground.

To make matters worse, the instruction I was given regarding the commands for the horses required me to make a 'kissing' sound for them to start and a blowing out of the lips to slow them down. I nodded sagely as Andrew Stone took me through the command signals for the horses. I didn't dare open my mouth because I wanted to save my lips for the take.

'Action!'

I managed to produce the starting command and off we went on our merry way. All went well for a while, and even Toralv – who had formerly expressed some misgivings about my ability to handle the sleigh – sang a carefree snatch of some Scandinavian melody.

As we approached the hill which preceded the sharp right hand bend, I attempted to blow out my lips in the slow-down signal. To my horror, I couldn't move my lips. At that moment it flashed through my mind that I had been warned that these old sleighs had no brakes.

I began tugging on the reins in a vain attempt at taking control, but the horses took no notice. Animals always seem to sense when an idiot is in charge of them. We went hurtling down the hill, rocking from side to side, and as we came to the bend, I managed to pull hard enough on the reins to swing the sleigh around. As I did so the runners on the right hand side hit a large boulder hidden in the snow. I let go of the reins and dived off my seat, taking poor Elizabeth Larner with me. Toralv and Florence jumped at the same time and, luckily, we all landed safely in a heap in the snow.

The horses went on in the direction of the stables in Lillehammer, galloping in step for the first time. On their way they ran into three parked cars, ruining the sleigh but fortunately doing no harm to themselves or any passers-by.

Andrew Stone had a few sarcastic things to say to me, and referred to me as 'Ben Hur' for the rest of my time on location. They had to re-shoot the sequence using a stuntman called Yakima Canutt, whose name I had seen many times on the credit list of Hollywood films. I was given a set of dummy reins while Yakima had to lie flat on some planks beneath our seats to steer the horses.

Filming was held up on several occasions, and to complicate matters a rift opened up between Virginia and Andrew. She had taken a fancy to a member of the crew and this caused so much trouble that a couple of executives flew over from Hollywood to try to restore some kind of harmony on location. A compromise was eventually reached and the couple promised to stay together until the filming was finished.

There is a funny, but poignant, footnote to the Stones' eventual split. When the filming was completed and everything was being wound up in Norway, the unit publicist, Eddy Kalish, received a telegram from Virginia asking him to send her the driving mirror from her hired Volvo, because it was in that mirror that her eyes had met those of her new man for the first time. I presume he was sitting in the back.

In the process of removing the mirror from the car, it broke in Eddy's hands. Undaunted, he bought another mirror from a Volvo dealer and sent that one off instead. 'If you've seen one mirror, you've seen 'em all,' was his motto.

I've never much liked looking at 'rushes'. The sight of myself on the big screen – and this film was being made for a *very* wide screen – always puts me off. However, one evening in Oslo I was persuaded to go along with some of the cast and crew to see the rushes at a cinema near our hotel. Unfortunately, they were to be shown without a soundtrack, so we watched our efforts in silence. Until, that is, one particular scene which involved the recital of some of Grieg's work in a concert hall.

The storyline was that some of the composer's friends had hired the hall in an attempt to secure financial backing for his work. Toralv, as Grieg, sat playing the piano while the characters portrayed by myself, Edward G Robinson, Florence Henderson and Elizabeth Larner sat in the almost empty auditorium. From time to time we looked around us and at each other, mutely expressing our disappointment at the sparcity of the audience.

The scene was quite a long one, with the odd re-takes being shown as well, and it suddenly occurred to me to liven up the proceedings by blowing a raspberry. Just after I had done so, the scene on screen showed Edward G Robinson looking at Florence Henderson with his eyebrows raised quizzically. This was followed by Elizabeth Larner giving me a questioning glance.

I could control myself no longer, and piped up from my cinema seat 'I didn't do it.'

Everybody at the rushes screening fell about laughing as our *Song of Norway* characters appeared to be turning around looking for the culprit who had farted. I was banned from attending the rushes thereafter.

I so resembled the character that I was portraying in the film, that children in the street used to run after me crying 'Bjornson!' when I was in costume. When we filmed on location in Bjornson's house, Andrew Stone allowed a genuine portrait of the playwright to remain in shot on a wall behind me in one of the scenes.

It was while we were filming in Bjornson's house that I received a message that an urgent phone call had come through from London. The telephones in the main house had been disconnected so that filming would not be disturbed, and the only working phone on location was in a lodge at the entrance to the property which was situated at the end of the long drive. As I made my way to the telephone it was snowing heavily and I must have resembled Captain Oates of the Antarctic as my mind raced wildly in frantic speculation about the nature of the call. Could one of the children be ill?

Could Myra have had a car crash? Every possible scenario went through my brain and by the time I reached the lodge I had turned into a snow-covered gibbering wreck.

I picked up the phone with trembling fingers. 'Hello?' I said tentatively. 'It's a Mr Milligan for you,' said the operator.

'Neddy! Will you record the voice of an elephant for me?'

'Yes,' I said. Milligan hung up.

On the long, cold trudge through the snow back to the house I thought of other things I might have said to him.

It was a rewarding experience to work with Eddie Robinson. He never seemed to be acting; every move, every piece of dialogue flowed naturally. I was surprised to discover that he was quite deaf. In one scene, we were sitting around a table in a piano shop along with Florence Henderson and a German actress who delivered her lines rather softly.

During the rehearsals Eddie found her very difficult to hear, and this made him late with his own lines. In the break before the actual take, he turned to me and whispered, 'When it's my turn to speak just tap me on the leg under the table.' This I did, but there was always a very tiny pause before he came in with his lines. Yet, when I watched the final result of the scene on screen it appeared that he was carefully considering what he had to say – and stealing the scene from everybody into the bargain.

Sitting beside him on the set was always a rewarding experience. He used to like telling us about his days with Warner Brothers when he and Humphrey Bogart took turns being the villain. Despite his tremendous success at playing gangster parts, he confessed that he hated firing handguns. Whenever he had to shoot at somebody, the make-up artist had to tape his upper eyelids back, because his instinctive reaction was to close his eyes every time the gun went off.

Eddie Robinson also revealed that Humphrey Bogart's

habit of snarling came from the fact that he suffered from heartburn. His condition caused him to take antacid tablets which left a chalky deposit on his teeth. Bogart attempted to remove this by moving his upper lip up and down over his teeth in his familiar 'snarl'.

Off screen Eddie was the exact opposite of the tough guy roles for which he was famed. He was a great collector of fine art, and when he had time off from filming he and his wife spent most of their time wandering around Oslo looking for new paintings. He was a gentle man and it was worth suffering the cold Norwegian winter to have had the privilege of working alongside him.

The film was not a great commercial success – indeed in one of the movie guides it is described as 'a bomb'. But nevertheless, I enjoyed the experience.

However, there is a sad footnote to *Song of Norway*. When the film came out, there were premières in Miami and New York and I was invited to the second.

It was a wash out in more senses than one because a torrential downpour hit New York that night and by the time I arrived at the cinema, after a horrendous journey through heavy traffic, Andrew and Virginia Stone, who shared the limousine with me were no longer speaking to each other. They were escorted up the sodden red carpet to the canopy in front of the cinema by a flunkey carrying a large umbrella. I followed behind umbrella-less, only to be accosted half-way by a drunk who seized the lapels of my dinner jacket and asked me for money. 'I'm English,' I said stupidly and that seemed enough reason for him to look for someone more affluent.

To judge from the audience I got a feeling that *Song of Norway* was not going to be another *Sound of Music*. Those of us who were members of the cast sat in the circle behind the row which contained the critics. When it came to the dinner party scene at Ibsen's house where Grieg suddenly says 'I must go back to my wife', and Ibsen stands up and says 'But not before you have played our new national anthem', a critic sitting in front of me put his head in his hands and groaned, 'Oh my God.'

Then I was *certain* that we were on to a loser.

When I arrived at Heathrow the following day, I was greeted by my manager Bob Kennedy with the sad news that my father had died. We had been expecting it to happen for some time. He had slowly become senile and we had been forced to put him in a nursing home in Ealing, near my brother's vicarage in Hanwell, and he had suddenly developed the pneumonia from which he died.

Even though I had come to terms with the fact that he could go at any time, it didn't really soften the blow when it happened. In his last days he didn't really recognize any of us, and so deeply embedded in his brain were the terrible experiences he had suffered during the First World War, that he believed he was back in the trenches.

He had been a good father to Fred, Carol and myself and when my mother was alive he was full of jokes and anecdotes about his life as a commercial traveller. His talent as an artist proved very handy as a supplement to his income, because he frequently drew cartoons for the South Wales *Evening Post*. After Mam died, he was like a lost soul. He spent his time visiting our families, and the sparkle had gone out of him.

The only 'Doctor' film I was ever in was also the only one of the series which did not make a profit. But my memory of the filming is clouded by tragedy. In the film, I played the part of a Pools winner who took a cruise on the strength of his winnings and became a target for the predatory Irene Handl who was looking for a rich husband for her daughter, Janet Mahoney. Leslie Phillips got into all kinds of trouble as the ship's doctor, and Robert Morley was the captain.

On the day that I was having a costume fitting for the film,

I had an urgent phone call from Bob Kennedy to tell me that Myra's mother had died suddenly.

It was a very dramatic scene that awaited me when I arrived home. At the time, Myra's parents, Flo and Jim, who lived in Swansea, were staying with us to help look after the kids, and I had received a request from the features editor of the *London Evening News* for Flo to be interviewed for a new series about comics' mothers-in-law. She had an angina condition for which she had to take tablets, and Myra was worried that the strain of being interviewed might be too much for her, but Flo said she would be all right.

When the reporter and photographer arrived at the house, Myra showed them into the lounge and introduced them to her mother. She then left the room and Flo sat down on the piano stool for the interview. The reporter had only asked her a couple of questions when she said 'Oh dear' and fell to the floor. Myra rushed in straight away and sent David to get Dr Unger-Hamilton who lived a few doors away. When he arrived, it was too late to do anything except place her in my study which adjoined the lounge, to await the coming of the undertaker.

There was not much that I could do to help except to offer comfort to Myra and poor old Jim who was stricken with grief. David was in a bit of a state – he was only a boy, and the shock of running for the doctor and then finding that it was too late to save his beloved grandmother remains with him.

Jim now came to live with us after the funeral was over and I'm glad to say that he lived on quite a few years after Flo. He was a lovely old fellow who was liked by everybody who knew him.

Life on a Main Road

For over thirty years we lived in a house on Cheam Road, between Cheam village and the town of Sutton. Our house stood in about an acre of ground between two side roads – York Road and Derby Road. A sturdy, detached house, the story goes that it was built in the 1920s by theatre owner and impresario Sir Oswald Stoll for his son. The front door faced a bus stop on the opposite side of the street and, after we had become established in the area, that particular bus stop became known as ' 'Arry's Corner' or 'Harry's House', depending on the social background of the conductor. From the top deck of a passing double decker it was possible to see right into our bedroom window, and I understand that the colour of my underwear became a general topic of conversation amongst those prurient passengers who happened to be sitting on the left hand side of the bus as it travelled past our house on the way from Sutton to Cheam. The name 'Flash Harry' was frequently mentioned, I believe, and I was not averse to a friendly wave.

The fact that everybody seemed to know where I lived in Cheam sometimes made us the target for eccentric behaviour. On one memorable occasion the household woke to find that someone had spray-painted the legend 'Harry Secombe is a wanker' on the wall outside the house. Between finding the graffiti and arranging to have it removed my knighthood was announced. The next day the artist added to his handiwork, which now read '*Sir* Harry Secombe is a wanker'. At least it showed he had some style.

One Saturday morning I decided to transfer a whole pile of books from my over-flowing library in the house to a mini-library I was setting up in what had been a garage alongside the property. This meant that I had to carry them out of the backdoor into the garden and through the door of their new home.

I had carried out two or three piles of books before I became aware of a girl's singing voice. At first I thought it was a radio somewhere, until I realized that the hidden singer would sing a phrase as I went from the back door to the garage door and, when I did the return journey, she would pick up from exactly where she'd left off. 'If I ruled the world every day would be the first day of spring . . .' accompanied one trip, and then on the way back, 'Every heart would have a new song to sing . . .' It occurred to me that at this rate, considering the length of the song, I could have removed half of Sutton Public Library before she had got to the reprise.

So, when I got back into the house, at the end of 'My world would be a beautiful place . . .', I tiptoed out through the French windows in the lounge, crept around to the front gate and peeped out towards the source of the singing. A young girl was crouched just below the wall, preparing to launch herself into 'Where we would dream such wonderful dreams . . .' as soon as I reappeared. She took a furtive peep over the wall, waiting for her cue, but, seeing me watching her from the gate, she gave a stifled scream and ran off. The poor girl was obviously auditioning for me, but I never found out what for.

*

For as long as I can remember, I wanted to be a writer. I was only good at two subjects in school, English and art, and I never, ever, unlocked the mysteries of mathematics.

My essays were much appreciated by one particular master, Mr Corfield, who taught English at St Thomas Elementary School. He used to make me stand up in front of the class and read my work out loud. This caused some jealousy among my fellow pupils and as a result I was often forced to defend myself in the playground. I found that the best way to do this was to try to get out of their way, and I spent many a playtime halfway up a drainpipe.

After I had left school I kept in touch with Mr Corfield, and maintained the contact through the war years, until our correspondence dried up. Then one day in 1956, when I went home to Swansea for a weekend during my first Palladium show, my mother told me that Mr Corfield was ill.

I went along to see him at his home just outside Swansea. By this time I had acquired some veneer of success, a big car, gold watch and suede shoes. As I entered his house I found him sitting by the fire in his armchair with a blanket over his knees. 'Hello Mr Corfield,' I boomed, a long way now from the spotty lad up a drainpipe.

Mr Corfield looked at me for quite a long time and then said, 'Harry, what went wrong?'

He stirred my conscience, though, and not long after I was invited to write something for a school magazine and I got the taste for writing all over again.

I had some short stories published in *Argosy* magazine and Spike asked me to do a foreword for a book he had written called *A Dustbin of Milligan*. The publisher was very pleased with what I had written and suggested that I should write a novel about show business. I replied that I was not sure whether I could do so, but promised that I would have a go at writing a first chapter and, if he approved, I would go ahead with the rest of it. His reply was most favourable and I resolved to finish the novel. Unfortunately a lot of other commitments got in the way and that first hand-written chapter lay forgotten in a drawer.

When Jennifer found it, years later, she said that I ought to finish it. I was afraid that it might not be a good idea, and anyway the man who had suggested that I wrote it in the first place was now with another publisher – Jane's Fighting Ships. My daughter has never been one for taking no for an answer and, without my knowledge, sent the material to Jeremy Robson who was just starting his own publishing company. He thought that it had the makings of a good book and offered me an advance and a deadline.

Faced with the incentive to work to a finishing date I went to Majorca and began writing. I had decided on a title, *Twice Brightly*, summarizing the content of the book which was about a comic's first week in Variety, having just been demobbed from the Army. I think I did most of the writing in three weeks, in longhand – the way I am doing this book – and Jennifer took it home to type.

By this time I was an occasional contributor to *Punch* magazine. The editor, William Davis, got Miles Kington, who was then the literary editor, to ask Prince Charles to review my book – the first time he had ever been asked to do such a thing. HRH complied and gave it a very flattering reception. His review began: ' "We would be delighted if you would write a review of Harry Secombe's first novel, *Twice Brightly*," was what the man from *Punch* said. "It doesn't have to be a comic masterpiece" (what does he mean, it doesn't have to be a comic masterpiece? People have wandered feet first into the Tower for less than that . . .)' But it went on to say, 'I was shaken with spasms of helpless mirth at frequent intervals.' And you can't get much better than that.

Other critics were pretty kind to me as well. Dennis Potter said that the novel was 'Very warm, very funny' and *The Times* called it 'a bright little novel'. For a week or two it was in the top ten bestseller list, which pleased both me and my publisher.

My next novel, *Welsh Fargo*, caused quite a stir not because of a Royal connection but in court circles of a different character.

The novel was all about a small bus company in South Wales run by a man called Dai Fargo whose bus is hijacked by an amateur gang of crooks. The title came from an ad lib by Paddy O'Neill on stage in the Palladium pantomime *Humpty Dumpty*. She suddenly pointed to me and cried, 'It's Welsh Fargo!'

It had no relation to anything that was going on in the scene and yet it got a laugh from the audience.

Thinking about it afterwards I had the idea of writing a book bearing that title, and I sort of worked backwards from there. Because I have the gestation period of a herd of elephants, it was many years later that the book eventually got written although I had mentioned the fact that I was in the process of working on it several times on various radio and television chat shows.

It came as a surprise therefore, that a solicitor's letter was sent to Robson Books complaining that a firm called Welsh Fargo Car and Van Hire in Bridgend, South Wales, was 'falsely and maliciously maligned' in my book.

I explained to my publisher that I had announced the title long before the plaintiffs had registered their business name. However, I offered to meet these people and to be photographed with one of their vans as a publicity stunt. They refused to do this and a writ was issued.

I was very sad that the case had to go to law, because we could all have benefited from a bit of good natured publicity over the affair. My publishers took legal advice, resisted the proceedings, and the plaintiffs withdrew.

Like most dilettante writers I sometimes feel uneasy in the company of those who do it for a living, although I had a good laugh at a telegram which Alan Coren sent to me from *Punch* on the occasion of the publishing of *Twice Brightly*.

'DEAR SECOMBE' it read. 'THIS IS A BLACK DAY FOR THE DEMARCATION INDUSTRY STOP WHERE DO YOU GET OFF TAKING THE BREAD OUT OF HUMORISTS' MOUTHS? IS THIS ALL THE THANKS WE GET FOR PUBLISHING YOU IN THE FIRST PLACE JUST TO KEEP YOU FROM SINGING AT LUNCH? OUR ADVICE IS TO STICK TO YOUR LAST ON THE GROUNDS THAT OLD COBBLERS NEVER DIE.

The *Punch* luncheons held at their offices in Tudor Street, just off Fleet Street, were always hilarious affairs and I was privileged to be a guest on many occasions. Some of the finest humorists in the country would swap anecdotes and insults around the famous *Punch* table. Clive James, Keith Waterhouse, Frank Muir, Alan Coren, William Davis, along with cartoonists like Geoffrey Dickinson, Wally Fawkes and David Langdon would submit famous political figures to good natured interrogation. I remember Edward Heath's shoulders heaving away, and, on another occasion, Jim Callaghan's robust laughter. After that particular luncheon I was pleased to give Jim, who was then in Opposition, a lift back to the House of Commons in my Rolls-Royce. The man at the gate gave me a startled salute. The next time I met him was when Myra and I were invited on board a Royal Naval frigate in Bridgetown Harbour, Barbados for cocktails. He was then Prime Minister and had been to a high-powered summit conference in Jamaica. It was the time when he returned home to turmoil and said, 'Crisis? What crisis?'

Incidentally, Ted Heath was also on board that evening and some of the press wanted a photograph of the two of them together. Jim was willing, but Ted demurred. Funny old world isn't it?

The eccentric behaviour outside the house was more than matched by what sometimes went on *inside* 129 Cheam Road, where we had four out of the ordinary children growing up.

Jennifer, our eldest, had an invisible alter-ego who was called Hellie Morgan. Heaven knows where Jennifer got the name from, but that's what she wanted to be called when she grew up. Jennifer used to tour with Myra and myself in my early pantomime and Variety days and mixed freely at parties. When she was four, Myra found her emptying all the glasses of wine when our guests had departed. It was a great way of getting her to sleep that night, but we discouraged her from doing it again. 'That's daddy's job,' explained Myra, looking at me in a knowing way. Jennifer has gone on to make her mark in Public Relations and now manages the Entertainment publicity team at BBC television.

Andrew was born at my parents-in-law's house in Swansea in April 1953. I was staying at the Averard Hotel in Lancaster Gate at the time he was born, and I was thrilled when Myra's Aunt Elsie phoned me with the news in the early hours of the morning. It was his arrival that spurred me into house hunting because, with two children to bring up, Myra and I decided that we had to have a place of our own. Which is why we finished up in Cheam.

He grew up to be a boy who was always wanting to be acting a part. At one time he thought he was Superman, and Myra found him on the garden wall with a towel pinned to the back of his shirt, holding the ends of the towel in his outstretched arms as makeshift wings. He was convinced he could fly and only Myra's intervention saved him from disaster. He developed a passion for playing the drums, which he used to practise in his bedroom, and his long-suffering mother used to have to take him and his percussion gear in her car whenever he had a gig at a friend's house.

He also had – still has – a dry sense of humour. One Sunday morning I decided to have a barbecue in the back garden. I had just bought all the equipment and was dying to try it out.

The barbecue consisted of a grill and spit mounted on four legs, and I set it up close to the kitchen window, filling it with charcoal. I had decided against using paraffin to get the fire going because I wanted to avoid setting the roof on fire, having once seen such a thing happen at a Sydney 'barbie' at which I was a guest. It had been an exciting evening and the presence of the Fire Brigade made the whole event 'go like a house on fire', as another guest wittily remarked.

Not having Sydney Harbour as a nearby source of water, I cleverly organized an electric poker with which to get the charcoal alight. The poker had to be passed to me through the kitchen window by Andrew and, when he plugged it in, I said 'OK, son, switch it on.'

Now, there just happened to be a loose wire in the handle of the poker, through which the house current passed on its way to my nervous system. The force of the electricity pulsed through me, making me jerk about like a marionette. I found that I could not let the damned thing go and, in between convulsions, I tried to tell Andrew to switch it off. He watched me leap about like a lunatic, thoroughly enjoying my antics, until, eventually, he got the message.

'That was very funny, Dad,' he said as he came out into the garden, still laughing. I showed him my burned hand, unable to speak after the shock. 'That's nasty,' he said. 'How did you manage to do that?'

He is now an actor.

Our youngest boy, David, was born in February 1962,

when I was at the Palladium in a revue *Let Yourself Go*, a
title that raised ribald laughter backstage when the news of
his birth came out. He was the first English-born child in the
family, having been born in Sutton Nursing Home.

His particular peculiarity as a child was his insistence on
wearing a German helmet at all times – until he was
persuaded that we had not lost the war. He started collecting
antiques at the age of nine, and was rarely seen without a
camera round his neck. At his prep school his headmaster
declared him to be a gifted child. He happened to be right,
because David has turned out to be a very fine photographer
and has taken photographs for many publications, including
the commemorative book, *Elizabeth R*, which involved him
travelling around with Her Majesty. He also has photo-
graphs in the archive of the National Portrait Gallery. To ask
him to take a family photograph for our Christmas card is
like using a sledge-hammer to crack a nut.

Katherine Sian arrived on 12 December 1967, just seven
days after *The Four Musketeers* opened at Drury Lane. Myra
was forty-three at the time Katy was born. She had to go into
St Helier Hospital for the delivery and, the morning after, the
gynaecologist said to her, 'Congratulations! You had the
only natural birth in the hospital last night.' Myra preened
herself. Then the tweedy lady doctor said, 'We old ones can
show 'em a thing or two, can't we?'

David was pretty miffed when Katy arrived. For weeks
before the event, he had convinced himself that the baby
would be a boy. He knew that the baby was in his mother's
tummy and he used to get Myra to open her mouth so that he
could shout down messages – things like 'You can have the
Action Man with the leg off,' or 'There's a German helmet
you can have when you come out.' He managed to work up a
smile when he saw Katy for the first time, but it was some
while before he forgave her for being a girl.

Katy was very aware from an early age that she was a girl

and played her feminine charm for all it was worth – even on the Almighty. When Myra noticed that Katy was not cleaning her teeth, she said, 'God will know that you haven't brushed them.' Katy went straight to the bathroom and attacked her teeth with vigour. When she came out on to the landing, she turned her face up to heaven, opened her mouth wide and proclaimed, 'Look God, I've cleaned 'em!'

Once, when I had arrived home after a trip to America, I went upstairs to have a snooze before supper and was soon flat out on the bed. Some time later, Myra asked Katy to go upstairs to see if Daddy was awake. She came into the bedroom, looked at my prostrate form and called down, 'I think he's dead.'

It was Katy who inspired me to write my first children's book one year when we were in Majorca. It was a very hot night and we were all sitting around on the patio fanning ourselves. Young Katy was on my lap, refusing to go to sleep until I told her a story. I was drinking in those days, and a couple of brandies after supper had loosened my imagination. I began to tell her about a monster who lived in the sea near the house and how Katy refused to be frightened by him – the *real* Katy wouldn't either – and they became great friends. Katy was asleep after about five minutes, but the rest of the family kept prodding me to finish the story. The following morning Jennifer said that I ought to write down the story and send it to my publisher. Eventually I did just that, and *Katy and the Nurgla* was born.

She used to spend a lot of time on her own, walking around the garden talking happily to her dolls, or conducting long conversations with invisible friends. It was obvious to me that she would want to be an actress, and so it proved.

There comes a time in a performer's life when he has to face the fact that his children will want to follow in his footsteps. The first thing that I said to Andrew – and to Katy when she got older – was that my profession was a tough one, that over ninety per cent of all actors were out of work at any one time and that the comfortable lifestyle that we had was because I had been very lucky.

In Andy's case, he listened to what I had to say and then invited me to see him in the school play. This was the moment of truth for me – if he was not very good, how could I tell him? I'd be doing him a disservice if I pretended that I'd liked his performance.

It was with fear and trembling that I went to see him in *The Boyfriend* at the City of London Freeman's School Hall. Myra and I sat holding hands tightly, waiting for Andrew's first appearance. I looked through the programme and whispered, 'At least they've spelled his name right.'

'Shhh!' said Myra.

My mouth was dry and my heart was pounding before our son made his first entrance. 'Please God, make him good,' I prayed silently. And to my great relief he was. The stage lit up as he came on, and from then on I kept turning round in my seat, proudly mouthing, 'That's my lad up there.'

When it came to Katy's turn to show what her potential might be, it was also in a school play. I could not be there for her theatrical début, but Myra said she could see straight away that Katy had star quality – even though she was wearing a papier mâché donkey's head.

Katy went on to Manchester University, where she got a 2 i degree in drama. From there she auditioned for the Bristol Old Vic Drama School and passed. At the end of her time there she won the Peter Ackerman Comedy Prize. She then joined Harrogate Repertory Company for a season and, to my great pride and pleasure, she shared the stage with me in *Pickwick* at the Chichester Festival Theatre in 1993.

There are two friends who played such big parts in my life that they almost became family. The first was Bob Kennedy, who I met many years ago when I played the Dudley Hippodrome, which he owned with his brother Maurice. It was a fine theatre with a very good reputation in the Midlands, but along with many Variety theatres it suffered when television took hold of the nation's entertainment needs.

The next time I met Bob was in 1960 when he was the company manager for the summer show I did at the Palace Theatre in Blackpool for George and Alfred Black. He had had to give up the Hippodrome because of lack of business, and was then living with his second wife Beryl and their baby daughter Sarah in digs in the town.

As it happened, Len Lightowler, who was my personal manager at the time, had some domestic problems and had decided to leave, so I asked Bob if he would like the job. He was delighted to accept and after the show finished in Blackpool he and his little family came down to live in Sutton.

They had been in Sutton for about a year when it was discovered that Bob had a brain tumour. It was operated on and, one day when he was still in hospital, Beryl brought little Sarah in to see him. He thought the baby was looking pale and suggested that perhaps she might be anaemic. Unfortunately it turned out that Sarah had leukaemia and, in spite of everything that modern medicine could do at that time, Sarah died. It was a terrible blow to them both, especially when it seemed that the tide was turning for them.

After his operation, Bob was left with a limp but he never let it get in the way of his work for me. His experience as a theatre owner made him invaluable to me as a personal manager and he was never at any time a 'yes' man.

We had a lot of laughs together and Beryl and Myra became great friends. Beryl had been a fine principal boy in pantomime and was full of funny stories about the business. She had also been in ENSA during the war, and the ship taking them to North Africa was attacked and sunk by a German U-boat off Algiers.

Bob travelled with me wherever I went and I particularly

remember a time at Los Angeles airport when his limp was getting more pronounced and we had a connecting plane to catch. We had very little time to spare to make the connection, so I bunged him in a wheelchair and raced through the airport, yelling like a banshee. He enjoyed every minute of it.

When we moved down to Willinghurst, Bob and Beryl came to live near us until, at the age of eighty, he died quite suddenly. He was still working for me until the day he passed on, and a kinder, more honest man I have yet to meet. After Bob's death, my secretary Julie Stephens managed my affairs for a while.

Another great friend for many years was Johnny Franz, who was the recording manager for Philips. I met Johnny as a result of changing recording companies after my contract with HMV was not taken up. I got an offer from Philips, and the first 78 rpm record I made was 'On With the Motley', with 'Recondita Armonia' from *Tosca* on the other side. To my surprise – but not to Johnny's – the record found its way into the charts.

I stayed with Philips for twenty-five years and through Johnny's choice of songs and some great orchestrations by Wally Stott and the great Peter Knight, I managed to pick up several golden discs and a couple of platinums.

With Johnny's help I made several albums abroad, one in Paris, another in Milan and a most memorable one in Vienna. It was recorded in the Mozart Concert Hall with the Viennese Concert Orchestra and featured a compilation of Tauber songs.

When I first entered the Hall I was very impressed by the place and the size of the orchestra. Johnny Franz was also nervous and so was Wally Stott, who was to conduct. I was introduced to the musicians with much formal heel clicking, and the first number to be recorded was 'Girls Were Made to Love and Kiss' by Franz Lehár. Wally tapped his music stand with his baton and off we went. After a few bars I lost my place in the music and automatically did what I always did at home when I made a mistake at a session: I blew a raspberry.

The orchestra skidded to a halt and there were questioning looks all around. For an awful moment I thought that I had really gone too far this time – desecrating this Mecca of Viennese music and ruining my own credibility as a singer. Then suddenly the lead trombonist blew a mighty raspberry-like beast on his instrument and the whole orchestra joined in the fun. It seemed as if they had been waiting to do that for years and the whole formal atmosphere changed. As I said to Johnny later, 'Welsh culture came to Vienna.'

One day Johnny rang me to tell me that he had a great song that he wanted me to record as soon as possible. I went along to see him and ran through the song with him. 'I don't think much of it, mate,' I said. 'But let's do it anyway.' And that was how I got to number one in the Hit Parade with 'This Is My Song'. Petula Clark got there first with the same song and for a while we were both in the top ten at the same time. This meant that I had to go on *Top of the Pops* with all the trendy groups. As I said at the time, it was like Ben Hur winning the Grand Prix.

When Johnny suddenly died of a heart attack, it was not long before Philips decided that we should part company. It was a pity because I had always enjoyed making records for the label, but it seemed that middle-of-the-road singers were on the way out. Ah well!

Life at Cheam Road was always eventful and, to add to the human menagerie, we also had a wonderfully eccentric cast of canine characters – one of which, our boxer Jim, only *thought* he was human.

I had bought Jim as a companion for Myra and the children when I was on tour and they were alone in the house. There was a kennels near to where I was playing in pantomime, and I went along to see some boxer puppies. I couldn't make up my mind which one to have, until we went into the farmhouse for a cup of tea and there, snoozing by the fire and surrounded by kittens, was this clown of a puppy.

'That's the one for me,' I said. 'He's obviously a character. What's his name?'

'Jim – just Jim,' said the lady, picking him up and handing him to me. He yawned sleepily and drew blood from my nose with his sharp little teeth. I had to buy him then – if only to get my own back when he got a bit older.

Of course, when I got him home he was immediately spoiled by the whole family, but, as he got older, his character began to assert itself in peculiar little ways. The back door, for example, he would protect against all comers – including us – but *anybody* could come in through the front door; if ever we wanted to move his great bulk from in front of the fire, we only had to say 'cats!' and he was off like a shot to the top of the garden, barking his head off at nothing. It didn't matter how many times we did this, he never cottoned on, though after three times in succession one cold winter's night his bark lost some of its conviction third time round and he gave me a harsh look when he trotted back in and slumped under the table.

When he was about a year old, I decided it was time to have him trained. He kept jumping up at people and licking them all over as they prostrate between his paws. This boisterous behaviour was costing us friends, so I took him along to a place where they sort out animal eccentrics.

As I left, a kennel boy was being dragged off his feet by Jim as he went for a startled retriever. 'They'll soon cure him of that,' I thought. 'When he gets home he'll be using a knife and fork.'

After the first week, we rang the kennels, as we were told to. 'He's quite a character, your Jim,' said a voice. 'We haven't been able to put him with the other dogs yet . . . but he is settling down.'

The next week we were told that he was still on his own and that he had killed a chicken. Four days later, we were asked to remove him because he was a bad influence on the other dogs.

I drove out to collect him and was expecting to find the place besieged by Jim leading a pack of savage hounds. It wasn't as bad as that. When the kennel boy brought him out he was pulled flat on his face by Jim's sudden joyous burst of speed on seeing me. I opened the car door, let Jim in and drove away with one hand, fighting off a happy, slobbering boxer with the other.

Although that was the end of his education, some of the commands he learned lingered on in a shadowy corner of his brain. Sometimes, when I said 'Lie down,' he might do just that. But he then would not get up until the next command unlocked his reflexes. 'Up!' I'd shout. No. 'Get up!' No. It was as if he was waiting for a password – sometimes in the middle of the road. 'Here boy!' Ah, that's it, and he would get to his feet and saunter on, exhausted with the mental effort of it all.

When he was eight the vet told us that Jim had a rare kidney complaint and had not long to live. This was terrible news, and in an effort to soften the blow of his passing, I went out and bought another boxer puppy – this time a bitch.

At first, we thought he would eat her. Having been master of the house for so long he resented the intrusion and nearly went mad with rage. Then he twigged that she was a lady and a new look came into his eye, he suddenly began to quite like the idea after all.

Cindy, the newcomer, was a born flirt and soon had him eating out of her paws. He looked like a big, stupid oaf, following her around the garden, his jowls drooling in

fervent anticipation. Soon there was no sign of the old Jim –
his coat was shining, his nose was wet and in six months he
was the father of half a dozen puppies. We kept the puppy
with the most laid-back personality, and Bella became a
much-loved member of the family.

Dear old Jim lived on for several years, happy with his lot,
until his kidney complaint eventually got the better of him.

Some years after Jim and Cindy died, Jennifer presented
Myra with a little Yorkshire terrier called Pudding, which
made up in character for what he lacked in size. He never
wanted to be treated as a lap dog and always adopted a pained
expression when he was petted and fondled. However, he was
determined to make his presence felt and was forever trying to
attract attention to himself. Sometimes, if Myra was looking
out of the bedroom window, he would growl to be picked up
so that he could see for himself what was happening. If
ignored, he would seize one of Myra's slippers in his mouth
and shake it as if he was killing a rabbit. This was his party
piece. Another favourite trick was to go into my father-in-law
Jim's bedroom in the morning and grab his false teeth – which
for some reason Jim kept in one of his slippers. This was
always guaranteed to get Jim out of bed to let Pudding out to
run in the back garden, where he had a secret rendezvous with
a large rubber ball to which he was strangely attracted.

He could always tell when one of the family was coming
home before the car entered the drive. When Andrew had a
motor bike, Pudding could recognize the sound of its engine
when it was at least a hundred yards away down Cheam
Road, and would start up a high-pitched barking which
differed in intensity from any other of the sounds he made.

Pudding never really got on with Schippel, a cocker spaniel
which was another gift from Jennifer, who was obviously
trying to set up an animal sanctuary in the house. Schippel
was named after the character I played in the film *The
Plumber's Progress*, but he was generally called 'Skip' by my

father-in-law, who could never manage the German 'schi'. Not that the dog ever noticed. Having been born on Hitler's birthday, he had the same propensity for ignoring what people said.

The two dogs had some kind of tacit agreement: Pudding ruled the area of the house above the stairs and Schippel was in charge of the ground floor. The funny thing was that whereas Schippel would grudgingly allow Pudding to come *down* the stairs, there was no possible way that Pudding would let Schippel *up* the stairs. Despite the fact that the spaniel was at least three times as big as the Yorkie, he was very careful not to upset him.

Every Summer for twenty-three years when we lived in Cheam, I used to recruit an all-star cricket team to play against the local eleven. The ground was just across from our house and, after the match, we held an open house party for both sides.

It was a thrill for me as captain to toss the ball to such great cricketers as Fred Rumsey or Eric Bedser and ask them to bowl. Sutton had a strong side and it was always fixed for them to bat first. They would knock up a reasonable score without losing too many wickets and when it got near to four o'clock, Ken Barrington would sidle up to me and say, 'I think it's time to get them out, maestro.' And suddenly there would be an extra bit of effort from the bowlers and, miraculously, the score would go from 200 for 3 to 220 all out by five past four.

When my side came in to bat, we would sometimes open with Peter May and Colin Cowdrey, who would produce some wonderful stroke play until it was time to let other batsmen come in, at which point they would give their wickets away like the great sportsmen they were.

My turn at the crease used to be about eighth wicket down and it was always arranged so that I scored the winning run. Sometimes it took a couple of cries of 'No ball' from the umpire as my wicket was flattened and a considerable amount of dropped catches by slip fielders who had suddenly developed butter fingers, before I managed to hit the ball that gave my side the victory.

The matches were always played in a great spirit of fun and the subsequent celebrations went on into the early hours of the Monday morning. Myra and her mother made sure that everyone had plenty to eat, while it was my job to tend the bar, a task I thoroughly enjoyed in those days. It was a tribute to the Sutton players that they accepted their yearly defeat with good grace.

During the time that I was president of the Lords Taverners, I was frequently asked to be Captain at cricket matches for charity events, and one such occasion took us to Bickley Park Cricket Ground in Kent. My team was called the Prime Minister's Eleven (Harold Macmillan being the Prime Minister in question) and we were playing against Len Hutton's side. The players included some show business stars, but the majority of players were top notch cricketers, including the likes of Colin Cowdrey and **Fred Trueman**.

On my way out to bat, I passed the Prime Minister sitting in a deck chair outside the pavilion. 'I'll do my best for you, sir,' I said. He nodded affably enough, but his 'sleeping tiger' eyes widened at my sartorial get-up. My woollen sweater had shrunk in the wash and clung to my very ample frame and my once white flannel trousers bore the marks of many diving attempts to catch the ball in the outfield. I was told later that Macmillan put his hat over his eyes as I waddled towards the crease.

At the opposite end of the pitch fellow batsman Colin Milburn, who was about the same size as me, but infinitely more athletic, gave me a cheery wave with his bat. He was at the receiving end, thank God, because the batsman I was replacing had been dismissed by the last ball of the over.

'Olly', as Colin was called by everyone who knew him,

faced the bowler with a grin. He could see that I was nervous because I had gone to join the umpire – I felt safer there. He whacked the ball through the covers and I was forced to run. Spectators later said that our running between the wickets registered seven on the Richter scale. Fortunately for me, Colin kept the strike for a couple of overs, by which time my spectacles had misted over and the plastic protector had slipped out of my jock strap to nestle against my left knee.

But, inevitably, it came my turn to face the music. Len Hutton, who was playing wicket keeper, threw the ball to Fred Trueman to start the new over. He then called all the fielders to get behind the wicket, leaving the whole pitch in front of me free, except for Olly. The crowd laughed as Fred strode purposefully to the boundary, rubbing the ball on his trousers as he went. He turned to start his run, pawing the ground like a Spanish bull. I could only just make him out in the distance and I turned round to Len Hutton and asked him what Fred was doing.

'Don't worry,' he said. 'Just stay where you are – Fred likes to have a bit of fun at the charity matches. He'll not hurt you, lad.'

Emboldened by this advice, I did a bit of play acting myself, taking up an elaborate attitude of waiting, tapping the bat on the crease. Meanwhile, Fred had launched himself into his run up, as the crowd roared in anticipation. I began to lose my confidence as his chunky figure powered towards the wicket.

'I've known old Fred for years,' I reasoned. 'He won't bowl the ball at me. He'll drop it as he gets to the wicket.' I was still praying that this would be the outcome when Fred bowled a full toss which hit me on my instep and shot off my boot over the boundary for four runs.

I hopped about on one leg a few times before dropping to the ground 'like a felled ox', as my manager Bob Kennedy later remarked in the pavilion.

They had to carry me off the field.

'That'll teach thee, lad,' said a grinning **Fred Trueman**.

There was no answer to that.

I noticed as I was carried past the Prime Minister that he had his hat over his face. I suppose it was the most diplomatic gesture Macmillan could make.

That wasn't the only time that Lords Taverners' events have got me into trouble. I once blotted my copy book when, as President, I made Margaret Thatcher the first Lady Taverner. The Lords Taverners had always been an all-male preserve and so at the reception on the Martini Terrace I referred to her as the 'thin edge of a delectable wedge'.

She completely misconstrued what I had said and went very red, saying 'I never considered myself to be a wedge.'

I think she must have thought I was referring to her shape. Afterwards I had to pin a diamond Lords Taverners' emblem to that formidable bosom under her eagle eye. I had the absurd notion that if the pin slipped there would be a huge bang and the Prime Minister would fly around the room like a pricked balloon. However, my trembling fingers did the job and I received a gracious smile, but for a moment there I thought I would have to hand back my CBE.

I have been Captain of the Lords Taverners' Golf Society for over twenty-five years, although I'm probably the most unsuccessful player of all time. The exception to this, however, was the occasion when I partnered Christy O'Connor Snr to victory, along with the gifted amateur Jack Cannon, in the first two-day Sean Connery pro-am tournament held in Troon in the early 1970s. The other two golfers didn't need me much until, by some fluke, I happened to hole out from a bunker for a net two on a par four and, for the first time in my life, I got a cheer from the crowd around the green. It helped our combined score to victory, even though I was out of contention for the last two holes. However, that was to be my only fleeting brush with golfing glory.

In all the times I have played in the Lords Taverners and *Sunday Express* Harry Secombe Classic, which is usually held at Effingham Golf Course in Surrey, I have never turned in a decent card at the end of the day.

I did make headlines one year though, an event I prefer not to remember.

It was on the first tee at Effingham. The Taverners Golf Committee are always very careful to put a warning notice in the programme of the day's play to the effect that spectators must keep their eyes on the ball when a player is driving off, to avoid serious injury to themselves. Some people who come to see the stars making fools of themselves on the golf course are not aware of the perils of the game – especially the children who come along with their parents.

On this particular occasion, I made great play of moving spectators away from both sides of the tee. 'I think you'll all be better off behind me,' I joked as I took a couple of practice swings at the starter.

I settled down and addressed the ball, then I somehow managed to slice the brand-new Dunlop 65 at such an acute angle that a lady who had heeded my jocular warning and positioned herself behind me, was struck on the head by the ball. The poor woman fell to the ground, bleeding profusely, and was taken off to hospital. I couldn't stop shaking all the way round the course, turned in a card that was even worse than usual and phoned the hospital as soon as I got back to the clubhouse. Fortunately, she had gained consciousness and was able to tell me not to worry, although she had to have eighteen micro-stitches in the wound. The least I could do was send her some flowers and my abject apologies.

The following day my photograph was plastered over the front page of the *Daily Express*, the picture having been taken by one of the staff photographers who just happened to be there waiting for me to do something stupid. He was right, I suppose.

The following year I invited the lady I had struck to attend the event as my guest. I made absolutely sure that she stood well away from the tee when I drove off this time.

Two years later, on the eighteenth green, retribution came when I was struck on the forehead by a bunker shot played by Air Vice Marshall Ramsey Rae – and a nicer fellow you couldn't wish to meet. I was too busy lining up a twenty-foot putt to notice that he still had to play a bunker shot. I saw double for a while and was made to lie down in the clubhouse. Everyone had a good laugh, of course, and the following year's programme carried a picture of me with my bump.

You will be pleased to hear that my younger son, David, is carrying on in the true Secombe sporting tradition. He once fractured his wrist in a school cricket match.

He was umpiring at the time.

When the buff envelope with the words 'From the office of the Prime Minister' came through the letter-box addressed to me in early May 1981, I opened it with trembling hands. The last time I had received one of these was when I was asked if I would accept the honour of a CBE. What if they wanted it back?

Then I read the words 'The Prime Minister has it in mind to put your name forward for the honour of a Knighthood in the Birthday Honours.' I let out a yell, the dogs started barking and soon the whole household was jumping up and down with excitement. Myra was in tears and David and Katy whooped with delight.

I then realized that I would be in Australia when the news came out and Myra would be unable to accompany me on the trip – she had to stay home to look after the kids. The other problem was that we had to keep the news to ourselves until it was announced on the date of the Queen's official birthday, and poor old Myra would have to keep the lid on the children's natural excitement for five weeks.

I was in Sydney the week of the announcement, and was due to open at the Parramatta Workers' Club on that very day. It would have been nicer perhaps and even grander to have been performing at the Opera House and I wasn't sure how to spell 'Parramatta' if I was asked to by some reporter on the phone from England. But new Knights have to put up with these matters – *noblesse oblige* and all that jazz.

The night before the news was released I went out with Jimmy Grafton and my Australian agent, Dennis Smith, for a celebration. I had already fielded a couple of phone calls from England that evening, in case I spilled the beans, forgetting that Sydney was eleven hours ahead of London. I was paranoid about having my title taken away by jumping the gun. The kids would never have forgiven me.

Having wined and dined unwisely the night before, I was woken in my hotel room by the room service waiter with my breakfast. As he stepped over the copy of the Sydney *Morning Herald* which had been pushed under the door, he looked down at my photograph on the front page alongside the news story of my Knighthood. 'What do I call yer now, mate?' he asked, dumping my breakfast tray on the bed.

I had a matinée at the Club that day, and the caterers prepared a huge spread of delicious seafood and a couple of bottles of champagne in celebration of the event. Jimmy Grafton arranged a press call and I felt I was walking on air when I went out on the stage for the first performance to the grand announcement of 'Ladies and Gentlemen – *Sir* Harry Secombe.' They were a great audience, they laughed at everything – especially when I sang – and I can't remember anything I said on stage. Despite my elation, I deeply regretted that Myra was not there to share the day with me.

She had troubles of her own at home. The day before the news came out she and Jennifer decided to prepare our housekeeper for the news. When she came in to work,

Jennifer sat her down in a chair and said, 'Now you mustn't say a word about this, but tomorrow Mum and Dad won't be Mr and Mrs Secombe any more.'

'Jesus!' she said, crossing herself. 'They're getting divorced.'

'No,' said Myra. 'Harry will be Sir Harry and I'll be Lady Secombe.'

The poor lady nearly keeled over and it took a large brandy to settle her down. When I eventually returned home, she dropped me a curtsey and called me 'My lord'.

It took Myra a long time before she got used to answering to 'Lady Secombe', referring to herself on the phone as 'Sir Harry's wife'. Then one day the man from Harrods, who was used to dealing with much more dignified titles than ours, came to clean the chandeliers in the lounge. He 'my ladyed' her so often she got quite used to the idea.

Some weeks before I was due to meet the Queen and receive the accolade, I was sent a letter from Buckingham Palace. It said, in effect, that some persons had difficulty in kneeling on these occasions and I was to answer the following question: 'Can you kneel?' I replied 'Yes' – refraining from adding 'but I can't get up again' in case I would have the honour withdrawn for impertinence. It worried me though, because I was at my heaviest at that time. 'Nineteen stone and two pounds' my bathroom scales indicated before expiring. Not *me*, the scales. Although I would have to lose some weight before *I* did.

The day before I was due to go to the Palace to receive the tap on the shoulder from Her Majesty, Myra and I were in the kitchen preparing lunch. Myra had the carving knife in her hand ready to carve the roast lamb, when she said 'How about a dress rehearsal?'

'OK,' I said, getting up from my chair.

'Kneel down, then.'

I knelt with some difficulty, and in the process of doing so, my trousers split from crutch to knee. I looked up at Myra, ashen-faced. 'What if this happens tomorrow?'

When Myra had finished laughing she said 'We can't have you making a "pubic" performance. Let's ring your tailor and get him to reinforce your morning dress trousers.'

He did, and as I walked forward to kneel before the Queen I had my fingers firmly crossed that John's strengthened stitches would survive. They held up beautifully, but I knelt so carefully that when I arose to have the badge of Knighthood put around my neck I could have sworn there was a twinkle in the Queen's eye.

When we first moved in to 129 Cheam Road it had the grand name of 'Chatsworth' on the front gate and I often wondered if the Duke of Devonshire ever received any of our mail by mistake. The fact that the house was in Cheam was a source of amusement for some of my show business acquaintances because of Tony Hancock's fictitious address – 23 Railway Cuttings, East Cheam. It proved to be a very happy house for us and, as my career advanced, we added to the property. We strengthened the fence around the garden and had a stone wall built in front of the house. The builder was Stan Wright, the husband of our first housekeeper, and the construction of the wall caused quite a bit of local interest. The stone came from the old Waterloo Bridge and proved to be extremely durable. The crossroads formed by the junction of Cheam Road and York Road on the right of us and its continuation into Gander Green Lane, meant that sometimes, particularly at night, the odd car coming out onto the main road would overshoot and collide with another vehicle passing in front of it ... The result was that one or other of the cars would finish up against our wall.

Around Christmas time, when the roads were icy and some drivers had taken a drop too much, our house had the appearance of a casualty clearing station. Myra said she was seriously thinking of putting up a Red Cross flag in the front garden. However, the wall stood up well to all the bashing it took, and I'm glad to say that it is still there today – even though the house has gone. We sold it in 1983 because, although we had been very happy there, the traffic noise was getting worse and Myra, who is at heart a country girl, longed to get away to where the grass was greener and the fumes were fewer. All our offspring were growing up: Jennifer had married and sadly divorced; Andrew had a bachelor pad; David was twenty-one and already standing on the edge of the nest flapping his wings; and Katy, at sixteen, was the only one still at school.

I was reluctant to leave the area when we had been so contented there – especially when the Secombe Centre in Sutton had been named after me and, in addition, I had been made President of St Helier Hospital's League of Friends. But, we were determined to make a move. We accepted an offer on our house, believing that it might be turned into a nursing home, and were given a year to find another abode. Now, that might seem enough time for anybody to spend looking for somewhere to live – but believe me it is not.

One thing we were sure about was that we did not want to move out of Surrey. It had become our home county for the past thirty-two years and we had no intention of looking elsewhere. That should have narrowed our choice down a bit, but it still took nearly twelve months before we eventually discovered what we were after.

Myra and Jennifer did most of the searching and I was only called upon for a second opinion if they were quite sure of a place. They looked at dozens of houses but there always seemed to be a drawback – either the place was in the wrong area, or a motorway was going to be built nearby, or it just didn't feel right – and we went off for a summer break still not having made a choice.

Then, out of the blue, we received a brochure on a house that seemed to have all the right requirements – in the countryside, with eight and a half acres of grounds and magnificent views across the Weald of Sussex to the South Downs. Those intrepid vetters of the estate agents' claims, Myra and Jennifer – this time with Katy – set out to see if this house would be what we wanted.

Fortunately – I say that because we were two weeks away from being homeless – they were ecstatic about what they found. I went along for a look myself and, while tramping around other people's houses looking at faults while at the same time nodding and smiling in apparent appreciation of what has obviously been a coal cellar airily described as a potential 'den' is not my idea of fun, I was really bowled over when I saw the place for myself. It was a listed house because of its architectural significance, having been designed by Philip Webb, a famous Victorian architect who was a great mate of William Morris and one of the Pre-Raphaelites, though I have to confess that I had no idea who he was until I looked him up in a reference book.

The deal was struck on the occasion of our second visit and we have never regretted it. To wake up every morning and see the view from our bedroom window is in itself well worth the price we paid for the house. Not a high rise building or an electricity pylon in sight all the way to the blue outline of the South Downs 'where every prospect pleases and only Man is vile', to quote somebody or other. We have great neighbours and have made many friends in the village, and we are determined that, God willing, we shall end our days here on the hill.

Pickwick and Other Musicals

I was relaxing on the beach in front of the Coral Reef Club in Barbados in 1962, thinking of nothing in particular, when Myra called me. 'Hey, look at this,' she said, waving a copy of the *TV Times*. 'Jimmy Grafton sent it for you to see.'

I took it from her and smudged a thumbprint of suntan oil on the cover photograph of myself dressed as Father Christmas. The shot had been taken during a photo call for an ATV Christmas Special I had starred in, which had featured the American singer Jo Stafford and was produced by Bill Ward. In the show I had played Father Christmas in one sketch and a Dickensian-type inn-keeper in another.

I lay back on the sun lounger and let my thoughts drift. I remembered fancying myself in the early nineteenth-century costume with the half-boots and John Bull-type hat. Someone had said 'You look just like Mr Pickwick.'

'Not a bad idea,' I thought as I slurped down another rum punch. *Oliver!* had opened in the West End and was proving to be a big hit. 'What's wrong with me doing Pickwick as a musical?'

By one of those fortunate coincidences, the playwright and author Wolf Mankowitz was coming to have lunch with us that day. He had just moved out to Barbados and he had not yet furnished his house. As he was an old friend, we had invited him to eat with us. 'We've got real chairs and tables in our hotel,' I said. 'It'll make a change from sitting on upturned crates.'

And so it was that over lunch I mentioned the idea I had for doing *The Pickwick Papers* as a musical. 'Great,' said Wolf. 'I'll do the adaptation.' Just like that.

When I got back to England, I told my agents, Jimmy Grafton and Frank Barnard, what I had in mind. They thought it was a good vehicle for me and got in touch straight away with Bernard Delfont. In no time at all Bernie had spoken to Leslie Bricusse about writing the lyrics and Cyril Ornadel about the music and *Pickwick The Musical*, began to take shape.

The Pickwick Papers is such an episodic novel – having originally been written by Dickens on a weekly basis for a magazine – that it was difficult to know how to whittle it down to a two-hour show. Eventually it was decided by the three collaborators to hang the central plot on the breach of promise action that Mrs Bardell took out against Samuel Pickwick.

Peter Coe, who had directed *Oliver!* was considered by Bernard Delfont to be the ideal man to provide the magic touch for our production. The casting was terribly important, and Peter had a great reputation for picking the right people. The eventual line-up proved that he had not lost his touch.

The three members of the Pickwick Club were to be Julian Orchard as Snodgrass, Gerald James as Tupman and Oscar Quitak as Winkle. Jessie Evans was to be my leading lady, Mrs Bardell, with Peter Bull as Buzfuz, Teddy Green as Sam Weller and a young, slim Anton Rodgers as Alfred Jingle.

Among the other members of the cast was Christopher Wray, playing the Fat Boy, who later became famous for his lighting emporium.

This was the first time that I had ever stepped out of my Variety character – no raspberries, no ad libbing – in other words, I had to concentrate on creating a Samuel Willoughby Pickwick who was as close to the role as Dickens and his illustrators had portrayed him. Fortunately I had the right build and with the aid of a bald wig and the brilliant costume designed by Roger Furze I managed to look very much like the old chap. I looked the part – now I had to prove that I could act it.

The rehearsals were an exciting time for all of us – and there was so much to be done. Marcus Dodds, the musical director, helped us learn the music. He had a great way with him, achieving the results he wanted with great good humour and patience, nursing the cast through Leslie's lyrics and Cyril's sometimes intricate music. From the start 'If I Ruled the World' appeared to be a big show-stopper, and so it proved on the opening night, but there were many other tunes which merited wider acclaim. 'There's Something About You' for one, which was sung in the ballroom scene, and 'Look Into Your Heart', a duet between Mrs Bardell and Mr Pickwick, which was played for comedy, but was worthy of a better fate.

The sets were by Sean Kenny who had created those for the stage version of *Oliver!* They were entirely different from anything we had worked with before and required quite a bit of getting used to. Every scene change was done in full view of the audience, with stage-hands in costume manipulating large wooden set pieces on wheels. The outside of the Fleet Prison became the inside of the prison and then metamorphosed into the George and Vulture without a curtain rising or falling. Some of us used to refer to it as 'open-cast acting' because of the stark nature of some of the sets – but it all worked magnificently. Peter Coe and Sean Kenny had collaborated on *Oliver!* – they knew exactly what they were doing and between them changed forever the old concept of stage design in the musical theatre.

The one thing which had me worried in those first days of rehearsals was the skating scene. I had never learned to skate, and as we were using a proper ice rink at the end of the first half, Peter Coe said that it was time I was given some lessons. I was duly sent off to Richmond Ice Rink with a pair of double-bladed skates, which did give me a bit more stability than the normal ones.

After a few lessons I was able to manage a couple of twirls around the stage ice rink, but I had a harder job learning how to jump off the ice on to a square of jabolite which concealed a padded trap cut in the stage into which I disappeared at the finale of the first act. Eventually I mastered the jump, but I don't think I ever landed in the trap without bruising some part of my anatomy. What with that leap and the cartwheel at the end of my duet with Sam Weller which came before it, I had Jimmy Grafton and Bob Kennedy searching the small print of my contract for a personal injury clause.

We opened at the Palace Theatre, Manchester – a venue which I knew well and where I felt comfortable – for a two-week try-out on 3 June 1963. I shall never forget the day that we heard the orchestra for the first time. We had rehearsed for weeks with just a piano, with all the usual stops and starts, and the choreographer, Leo Kharibian, shouting out the rhythms. 'Come on, come on – one, two, *three*, four.' After a while the music begins to take second place to the action in one's mind. Then came the time for the orchestra to take over. We all sat in the stalls crossing our legs and our fingers in an agony of anticipation.

When the music started up there was a collective sigh of relief as the tunes we were getting rather fed up with began to take on a new life. Brian Fahey's arrangements breathed the very spirit of the times of Dickens. No strings, plenty of brass and percussion for the jaunty pieces, and muted for the prison scenes. By the time that first full band call had finished some of us were in tears and some of us were laughing but all of us were delighted with what we had heard. I think we all knew then that we were involved in something big.

The first night Manchester audience loved the show. The performance was for the Variety Club of Great Britain and quite a few fellow actors were out front. When they came backstage afterwards the verdict seemed to be that I had passed my acting test.

By the end of the Manchester run, most of the rough edges of the show had been polished and Sean Kenny's sets weaved in and out of the action with amazing precision. Peter Coe had given us all copious notes on our shortcomings, Leslie Bricusse and Cyril Ornadel were very supportive throughout rehearsals and Marcus Dodds's equanimity remained firmly in place. Bernard Delfont pronounced himself pleased with our efforts. All we had to do now was face the ordeal of the West End first night.

The London theatre we were to occupy was the Saville, which though not in Shaftesbury Avenue, was a venue with a good reputation. The opening night was, to our relief, a huge success for all of us. As Julian Orchard said to me after the curtain came down, 'I think we can safely send our laundry.'

The press reviews the following day were generally highly favourable. 'A miraculous *Pickwick*', announced Milton Shulman in the London *Evening Standard*, going on to say, 'I think that the book by Wolf Mankowitz has made a reasonable stab at retaining the spirit and feeling of this comic masterpiece.' He had some favourable words to say about Sean Kenny's sets too: 'Manipulating a number of wooden units as if they were part of a series of gigantic jigsaw puzzles, he can transform the Fleet Prison into the

The Queen looking radiant. I think it was something Myra said.
(*Joe Matthews*)

Outside Buckingham Palace in 1963. Andrew and Jennifer check if the
CBE is gold. Unfortunately, it is not.

With Harold Macmillan. He said 'Say something to make me laugh.'
I said 'The Liberal Party.' He laughed. (*Associated Newspapers*)

Tommy Cooper, me and Cardew
Robinson at a cricket match. I was
the heavy roller.

My manager Bob Kennedy in a
helicopter. He was glad to get out.
(*Paul F Cooper*)

My mum and dad at my first *This Is Your Life* in 1958 with Eamonn Andrews. (*BBC*)

My favourite picture of me and the missis, doing a Fred and Ginger impression.

Me and Jim. Jim is the intelligent-looking one.

Jennifer, Myra and Andrew teaching me to read.

Early Victorian-type family portrait with a recalcitrant Andrew.
(*Sunday Mirror*)

Katy's first day at school and my second.

With my dear mate Roy Castle, as Laurel and Hardy. (*Radio Times*)

Johnny Franz and me at a Philips recording session.

Variety Club Luncheon to celebrate my twenty-fifth anniversary in show business. With Arthur Askey, Hilda Baker, Spike, Eric, David Kaye and Jimmy Tarbuck. (*Press Association*)

Signing session for my first novel, *Twice Brightly*. The lady next to me bought two, one for each eye.

With Ronnie Cass on *Highway*.

Dame Thora and me together on a *Highway* from Morecambe. We had
called a truce in our Sunday programme war.

Pickwick, Chichester 1993. This time I don't need a bald wig. (*John Timbers*)

Katy on my shoulders at Margate. (*Daily Mirror*)

George and Vulture Tavern during the singing of a few bars of music and the tavern can become a frozen pond fit for ice-skating during the speaking of a few snatches of dialogue.'

Of my performance, Shulman was very kind indeed

It was pretty obvious by the second and third weeks of the run that we were in for a pretty long spell at the Saville, and so it proved. The Saville Theatre became my home from July 1963 until February 1965 and a very happy home it turned out to be. We all got on very well together as a company and every month I would hold a 'Harry's Happy' party in the downstairs bar. I happened to have a 16 mm projector complete with sound, and the week before the party I'd circulate catalogues of films for hire and we'd all vote for the one to be shown on the night. Most of the films chosen were either musicals or those with a showbiz theme and they were all greeted with cheers and applause as if we were watching them live. In the time taken to change reels we'd all have another glass of red wine or a chicken leg from the buffet laid out on the bar counter. I have never since enjoyed films as much as I did then.

Julian Orchard was a particular pal of mine. He was over six feet two and when he wore his top hat he simply towered over me. The character of Snodgrass ideally suited him; it allowed him to employ wonderfully exaggerated gestures as he attempted to woo the Wardle daughter, Isabella, with his execrable poetry, and his attempts at dancing in the ballroom scene were a joy to behold. We had a lot of laughs together during the run.

All the cast, without exception, were the Seymour illustrations brought to life – Oscar Quitak was the perfect Winkle, the timid sportsman; Gerald James as Tupman, the romantic middle-aged suitor to the spinster Aunt Rachel Wardle could not have been bettered, and Anton Rodgers was the personification of the loveable rogue Jingle. Perhaps the most terrifying character of all, Mr Buzfuz, was played by an actor who was the living image of the man in the original drawings and yet was the gentlest and nicest person one could hope to meet, Peter Bull. He looked so fierce that sometimes at matinées children would cry out in fear as he delivered his speech in the courtroom, but I could reduce him to a giggling wreck with no bother at all. Teddy Green, a fine dancer and singer, was the first of three Sam Wellers in this particular production. We had a great rapport both on and off stage and I was sorry when he left the show to join another musical called *Baker Street*. He was succeeded by his understudy, Norman Warwick, who did a very good job for the last few weeks of the London run.

There were, of course, hitches in the show during such a long run – the scenery would sometimes become snarled up as the various trucks collided with each other in the dark. On one particular occasion about four weeks after we had opened, I had a rather nasty shock myself.

Right from the start of the show, I was always afraid that I would forget the first two verses of the introduction to the song 'If I Ruled the World'. The words were tricky because they had to be sung with a sense of urgency. In the scene just after the opening of the second half, Pickwick becomes caught up between the rival factions in the Eatanswill election. He is mistaken for Mr Slumkey, one of the candidates, because he happens to look like the picture of him, as depicted on a banner being carried by a Slumkey supporter. Despite Pickwick's protestations, he is lifted on to a balcony, while the crowd – who assume he is Slumkey – demand that he makes a speech. Pickwick reluctantly launches into, 'Friends, dear friends, may I say I'm not a politician, A simple minded, silver-tongued magician, Whose words, fine words, could charm the very birds from the trees with ease. Please, dear friends, though I may not be the world's physician, By nature I'm of modest disposition,

Suppose you chose, instead of men like those, Men like these – and these. Men who want a world that's fine and free. Men like Nelson, Wellington and Drake and me. We want a world our children will be proud to see. And if I had the chance, I know just how it would be . . . If I ruled the world . . .' etc.

I had always had difficulty in remembering the words, as a precaution, just before the dress rehearsal I wrote the first two verses in biro on the plain wooden bar on the balcony upon which I stood to deliver the song. After a week or two I didn't really need the words, except as a safety net to glance down and check they were there. One Monday night, I could smell fresh paint as I entered the theatre and was told that the scenery had been freshened up over the weekend. I thought no more about it until the moment came when I was thrust up on to the balcony for 'If I Ruled the World'.

'Please, dear friends,' I began, waving my arms at the company, who were now in front of me facing upstage. 'May I say ...' I looked down, as was my habit, to check the words only to find that they had been completely obliterated by the painting.

My mind went blank as the relentless bolero rhythm commenced in the orchestra pit. I knew that I had to say something vaguely political, so I gabbled away insanely over the music, speaking utter rubbish.

Below me the cast were in hysterics at my antics, knowing that the audience could only see their backs. Fortunately the music for the verses was soon over and the tune came to the 'If I Ruled the World' part, which the company joined in singing to help me out.

I was still shaking at the end of the performance, and when I was told that an old army mate was at the stage door, I was half inclined not to see him. 'Oh, all right, let him come in,' I said, preparing my excuses for cocking up my big number.

'Great show, boy,' said Emrys Evans, ex-Bombardier.

'That "If I Ruled the World" was magnificent. I had a lump in my throat when you started singing that, very moving.'

I could only bow my head in thanks, not trusting myself to speak.

'That first bit was very political, though. I didn't know you were a socialist.'

'Neither did I,' I said.

Later in the run, that same balcony was the setting for a far more poignant moment in my life. For some weeks I had been aware that my mother was losing her battle with cancer of the bowel and Myra and I had driven down to Swansea to see her every Sunday. On the last Sunday before she died we were all at her home, sitting around her bedside laughing and joking about the fun we used to have in the old days. Talking about the way Dad had to take a chair on stage whenever he had to do his party piece, 'The Wreck of the 11.69', a parody of a railway accident. He was so nervous that he used to grip the back of the chair like grim death during his performance. And that was the cue for the story of how I used to entertain the family on a Sunday evening after church at Gran's terraced house in Danygraig. My nervous disposition would only allow me to sing if I could not be seen, and so I would sit on the outside toilet with the door open, surrounded by squares of newspaper stuck on a nail, and from that uncomfortable wooden seat I would belt out my favourite hymns while the rest of the family gathered in the nearby kitchen to listen. Mam always used to love telling that story.

We all knew that she did not have long to go and there were tears mingled with the laughter as evening came. When we left for London the following morning, there were lingering good-byes and a tacit acceptance that this would be the last time we would see her. My sister Carol had been wonderful throughout Mam's illness and was staying with her to nurse her until the end. Brother Fred was, of course, on hand with comforting words, but poor old Dad seemed bewildered and lost.

It was agreed between us before we left that I was to stay up in London if anything happened before the next weekend, but I would fly down for the funeral.

When the news came that Mam had died, I had to go on stage as usual, and managed not to let my grief show until the time came for me to get up on that balcony to sing 'If I Ruled the World'. As I climbed up the steps I was thinking that if I *did* rule the world my mother would still be alive, and I began to shake as I started to sing the first couple of lines. Before me, the whole cast – who knew what had happened – willed me with their eyes and gestures of encouragement to get through the song. Thanks to that wonderful bunch of people, I did, but I was grateful that I had ten minutes to myself before I had to get back on stage for my next scene.

As arranged, Myra and I flew down to Swansea for the funeral in a chartered aircraft, landing at Fairwood Common – a small airstrip quite near where Myra's parents lived. The service was held at St Peter's Church in Cockett, where my brother Fred was the vicar. The church was packed with family and friends, and there were quite a few people outside the church, genuinely sympathetic for the family's bereavement and not out of a morbid desire to see Harry Secombe's mother's funeral. Mam was such a well-loved figure in the community that she was mourned for the person she had been and for the good that she did in her life, not for having a son in show business.

After the burial ceremony we all went back to the house for tea and sandwiches and the conversation was all about the joy that Mam had brought to us and the fun we had shared as a family. Everyone knew how much pain she had been suffering and the phrase 'a happy release' was the verdict of the day.

On the plane trip back to London I felt much calmer now that the service was over, and though I dreaded the evening performance, I got through it without too much trouble. The sensation of my mother being somewhere around me was most comforting and the combination of that feeling together with great support from the company made 'If I Ruled the World' less of a minefield for me.

Towards the end of the run at the Saville, Jimmy Grafton told me that Bernard Delfont was negotiating with the American impresario David Merrick for a tour of the United States, with a view to a Broadway presentation. This was exciting news for the company when Peter Coe gave out the news on stage. Thanks to the influence of Equity, we were going to be able to take quite a few of the cast. Of the Pickwickians, Julian Orchard and Oscar Quitak were coming. Peter Bull as Buzfuz was to join us later and Anton Rodgers was to rejoin the company to play Jingle. Also included were Tony Sympson and Michael Derbyshire, who played Dodson and Fogg, and Michael Logan who took the part of Wardle. Gerald James had already left to join Olivier's National Theatre company. We were to have a new Sam Weller – a young lad called Davy Jones who was already over in America having just finished playing the Artful Dodger in *Oliver!* on Broadway. But, before *Pickwick* reached Broadway, Davy was replaced by my old mate, Roy Castle.

David Merrick came over to London to see the show and to see for himself what he was going to be promoting. A slim gentleman with a dark moustache and the air of a man who was serious about money, his reputation went before him, and those of us who had been advised of it were pretty wary in his presence.

At one time, after some bad critiques of one of his Broadway productions, Merrick had banned all critics from seeing any of his shows. Instead, he found individuals who happened to share the same names as some of the 'Butchers of Broadway' – as the New York theatre critics were called –

and got them to make complimentary remarks about the show. These quotes were then displayed outside the theatre to the amusement of the whole of show business and the chagrin of the critics, who could only grind their teeth in frustration when they read the sweet congratulatory words contributed by their namesake reviewers.

Merrick was also reported to have a low opinion of actors, although I have to say that he seemed to like me and always came backstage to my dressing-room when we were on tour in the States. Before he left the theatre the night he came to see *Pickwick* for the first time at the Saville, he put his arm around my shoulders and said that I was the 'eighth wonder of the world'. I wondered at the time whether I came before the Pyramids or after the Hanging Gardens of Babylon, but I didn't think I ought to ask.

After the show closed in London, it was decided that I would spend a few weeks on holiday in Barbados before we opened again in San Francisco, which meant that I would arrive after the other members of the company, who were to start rehearsals with the American cast.

Myra and I arrived along with our younger son, David, and Bob and Beryl Kennedy at San Francisco Airport full of excitement about the forthcoming opening night. At least the others were – I was quietly dreading the moment.

We booked into a Hawaiian style hotel on Clay Street and I remember standing outside our room that night looking at the lights of the big city and wondering what the hell I was doing there. Myra came and joined me. She took hold of my arm and said, 'Hey, you're shivering. Are you cold?'

'No,' I replied. 'I'm frightened.'

'You'll be all right, love,' she said. 'You wait and see.'

'God, I hope so.' I looked up at the stars, addressing him directly.

The following morning was the time for me to meet the whole cast and orchestra for our first orchestral run-through.

Bob and I went along to the Hertz Rent-a-Car office to pick up the Cadillac I was hiring for our seven-week stay in San Francisco. It was an enormous yellow convertible and I sat in the driver's seat with some trepidation. From what I had seen of the lay-out of the city's streets, it was not going to be an easy first drive to the theatre. It took me ten minutes before I could find the 'hand' brake – it was one of those pedals that you release with your foot. Bob and I were both too proud to go back into the garage and ask the Hertz representative how it worked, as I had airily assured him that I knew how to drive the car, not realizing that there was no handbrake as I knew it. Eventually, after going through the driver's handbook, Bob discovered the secret.

To make matters worse, I decided to take what the map called 'the scenic route'. This was a great mistake. I found myself unable to turn off the freeway out of the city and was forced to drive across the Golden Gate Bridge in the opposite direction to where we were supposed to be headed. Eventually I found a place to turn around, but by this time we were already half an hour late for the band call.

I have always prided myself on being early for appointments, especially when meeting people for the first time. And now, here I was, pulling up outside the Curran Theater over an hour late. Bob went off to park the car – I never expected to see him again – and I went in to face the music, and the musicians, to say nothing of the new members of the company, some of whom adopted elaborate attitudes of waiting, looking at their watches and heaving sighs.

My abject apologies were readily accepted by the English production members who were getting fed up with making excuses for me ... 'He's never late ... Perhaps he's been kidnapped', etc. As I was introduced to all the new actors, I noticed a wariness in their manner, something I had come across some years before when I had met the orchestra for the first time at the band call for an Ed Sullivan television show in New York. It seems that until you have proved yourself, until you have shown them what you can do, American showbiz folk reserve their judgement. I don't think it's really a bad attitude – it certainly puts you on your mettle. And so, when the time came for me to sing the Christmas number in the opening, I gave it all I had. My voice was in pretty good shape after the holiday in Barbados and it was a great feeling to be back in harness again. The musicians in the orchestra nodded approvingly and my lovely Saville cast members turned to their new American colleagues to smile knowingly as if to say 'We told you he wasn't too bad'.

Fortunately the conductor, Ian Fraser, was a Scotsman, and he too seemed to heave a big sigh of relief as he brought his baton down at the end of the number. 'Well done, mate,' he said with a grin and I knew then that I had a friend in the orchestra pit. My fears of a potential disaster on the opening night were at least lessened. All I had to worry about now was where Bob had managed to park the car.

The new Mrs Bardell was Charlotte Rae, who was known to American television audiences as the wife of the policeman in the comedy series *Car 54 Where Are You?*, and the American Tupman was John Call. Davy Jones as Sam Weller was always full of life and we got on like a house on fire. I never quite knew what he was going to get up to on stage, which made a change because I was the one with the reputation of being somewhat unpredictable.

There was another member of the team I was glad to see. Gillian Lynne, with whom I had worked in the pantomime *Puss in Boots* in Coventry, had joined the company as choreographer. She was already building a tremendous track record in her field and had a great reputation for getting good results.

Rehearsals started in earnest and the newcomers soon got into the swing of things under the combined direction of

Peter Coe and Gillian. David Merrick insisted on some new scenes being added and new songs were also tried out. This happened all the way through the tour across America and was a constant source of friction between Peter and Merrick. I was on Peter's side – going along with the principle of 'if it ain't broke, don't fix it'.

Bernie Delfont sent over to England for Keith Waterhouse and Willis Hall to provide some extra material. They stayed for a couple of weeks, but in the end very little of what they had written was used. Leslie Bricusse was staying at the same hotel as ourselves, and every day he sat around the pool scribbling away on a writing pad, trying to keep up with Merrick's demands.

The Curran Theater was an old fashioned building, not unlike those in the West End, and I felt quite at home after the first couple of rehearsals there. The theatre had an intimate atmosphere and the acoustics were good, something which was always of concern to me.

The dress rehearsal went very well, or so I thought, until the theatre manager came into my dressing-room afterwards and said 'Great, Harry – but what the hell were you saying? You were talking so quickly I couldn't understand a word.'

I should have realized that whereas a British audience understands most of the dialogue spoken by American actors due to years of watching American movies, the reverse did not apply. The majority of UK films only played the art house cinemas in the States and the only English accents the American cinemagoers recognized were the mid-Atlantic speech of the likes of Ronald Colman, C Aubrey Smith, David Niven and Greer Garson – British actors who lived in Hollywood. Any other British accent was difficult for them to pick up. My own version of the character Pickwick was a hint of Bloodnock from the *Goon Show* with strong overtones of my Welsh upbringing. In addition, I have always had a habit of speaking rather quickly.

I took the manager's advice and slowed down my dialogue so much that I put about ten minutes on the show. (It made me laugh later when one critic referred to Davy Jones's 'Cockney' accent. Davy hails from Manchester and never attempted to speak anything other than pure Mancunian.)

When opening night came, I remember sitting in the Curtain Call Bar across the street from the theatre about two hours before the show having a drink with Bernie Delfont, Jimmy Grafton and Bob Kennedy. It was too late to do anything more to the production and, as Jimmy said, 'It's all in the lap of the Gods . . .'

'And, of course, the stalls and the circle,' added Bernie, who was more practical.

My career was on the line and Bernie's trust in me to succeed was also going to be tested. We all shook hands quietly and, as we crossed the street back to the theatre where my name was now in lights, I thought of my usual reminder to myself on these occasions. 'Don't forget there are a hundred million Chinese who neither know nor care that you are going out front tonight.' Then I remembered that San Francisco had about the biggest Chinese population of any city outside China.

When I entered my dressing-room it was full of flowers and cables wishing me well from Myra and the kids, members of the company and all my mates back home. My Scottish dresser, David, was in the kilt and sporran he always wore on first nights and he too was in a fine old state of excitement. He had been in the chorus of many West End musicals as a young man and was always very nervous on first nights. There was a cup of tea waiting for me and he had already begun to arrange the flowers I had received.

The 'half-hour call' came over the tannoy system and I started to climb into my costume. As I did so, a calm came over me and I began to look forward to the performance.

Myra was the last one in the dressing-room to wish me good luck and I think she was more nervous than I was now that I had settled down. She knew more than anyone else what was at stake for both of us, and the knowledge that she would be out there in the audience rooting for me gave me added strength.

For the last fifteen minutes I had the dressing-room to myself. David knew that I liked to be quiet before I went on stage and discreetly left the room to be on hand side-stage. I paced up and down like a caged lion for about five minutes, psyching myself up for my entrance, until the 'overture and beginners' announcement came over the speaker. 'It's too late to go home now, Harry,' I told myself, and walked down the steps to the stage.

'Break a leg, folks,' I said to the assembled company, all set for the opening. Then the curtain rose and we were off . . .

To my great relief – not to mention that of Bernie, Jimmy, Bob, the theatre management and, last but by no means least, Myra – the first night performance of *Pickwick* in America was a huge success. After the final curtain, Jimmy, Bob, Myra and I huddled together in my dressing-room, crying unashamedly, so strong was our collective emotion. I can say, quite honestly, that I have never cried like that before or since.

The reviews were pretty good for the show, although one Oakland newspaper referred to the author as 'Chuck Dickens'.

As a family we had great fun driving around Northern California at weekends, although the streets of San Francisco were quite frighteningly steep. I remember one particular time when I stopped at a traffic signal and was unable to see over the bonnet.

I found the people of San Francisco very hospitable and one resident in particular became quite a chum. His name was Lou Luhrie, a great theatre buff and a man of considerable influence in the city. His life was a typical 'rags to riches' story. As a boy he had sold papers on a Chicago street corner outside a large building which he swore that he would one day own. He made his money during the Klondike gold rush – not by digging for the precious metal, but by selling the miners the tools with which to prise it out of the ground. Consequently he made a fortune and acquired a lot of real estate in San Francisco as well as the building in Chicago he had promised himself he would buy.

Lou used to host a lunch party once a week at Jack's Club to which many of the most influential politicians in the city were invited. I had an open invitation from him because he loved *Pickwick* so much. As it happened, I had a couple of Dickens' original letters with me which I had brought to the States for publicity purposes. I gave him one of them and he was overwhelmed by my gesture. This was probably because Lou was more used to giving than receiving, a trait that I have found in many wealthy Americans – great givers but somewhat bewildered recipients.

Myra, Jennifer, Andrew and David saw quite a bit of San Francisco while I was working. It was the 'flower power' era and there were some rather weird looking people wandering abroad in those days. A few weeks into the run Myra and the children had to go back home so that Jennifer and Andrew could return to school. It was very lonely without them and weekends saw me driving the big Cadillac up to the Yosemite Valley or down to the Big Sur country with my faithful manager Bob beside me, covering his eyes as I manoeuvred the hairpin bends.

Pickwick's next venue was the Los Angeles Music Center where ours was only the second show to be staged. It was a wonderful theatre with a huge auditorium and a stage that was so large that our sets were dwarfed. When the manager showed me around on the first day of rehearsal I said 'If we get the bird here, at least it'll be a peacock.' He looked at me strangely, crossing himself at the thought. There was little chance of *Pickwick* being a financial flop because most of the seats had been booked well in advance, but we were still an unknown quantity as far as Los Angeles' audiences were concerned.

On the first night, before the curtain went up, I spent my quiet moments in my capacious dressing-room reading some of the first night telegrams, and was delighted to find one from Bob Hope saying 'Welcome to Piccadilly West'. That cheered me up no end, and I went down to the stage for my entrance feeling a little less nervous because of his kind gesture.

The show went very well – perhaps not quite as well as San Francisco because we all felt a bit inhibited by the size of the stage and the number of film stars in the audience, but we had good reviews from most of the critics and settled in quite comfortably for the eight week run.

During this run Myra and the children came back out to join me. We stayed at the Hollywood Hawaiian Hotel – a nice little motel on Grace and Yucca, not far from Sunset Boulevard. The hotel pool was very welcome in the hot climate, and the fact that the children could splash around in the water took a lot of the pressure off Myra. There was a supermarket quite close to the motel where Myra used to shop. I'll never forget one afternoon when she returned from a shopping trip looking quite upset. She is dark-haired and brown-eyed and with her vivacious personality and lilting Welsh accent she has often been mistaken on our travels as a native of Spain, Italy, Greece – and even Fiji! As she was paying at the supermarket check-out for her purchases – which included a large melon – the man at the till enquired, 'Persian?'

'No,' replied my wife, dimpling prettily. 'I'm Welsh.'

'Not you, lady, the melon,' replied the man tersely.

There was a Lions Club International Convention being held in Hollywood at the time and we were all surprised one morning to find the pool full of Eskimos. It was no surprise to me, though, that they assumed Myra was one of their ilk.

Our younger son, David, was just four years old at this time. He had watched so many Westerns on American television that he had taken to wearing one of my suede trilby hats and had affected a limp in a fair impression of Walter Brennan. He also made a firm friend of the hotel's short order chef, imitating his cries of 'two eggs over easy' or 'two eggs looking at you', and became a great favourite with the staff at the hotel – at least, that was what they claimed.

At weekends we went on many sightseeing trips to places like Santa Monica, Carmel, Palm Springs, San Diego – all places I had seen in American films or read about in movie magazines as a boy and was determined to visit while I had the chance. It was an exciting time in the theatre, too. Stars of the calibre of Jack Benny, Jim Backus and Claire Trevor came backstage to meet me and the great film director Mervyn LeRoy asked me to meet him at Universal Pictures Studio to discuss a project in which he thought I might be interested.

It was a good idea. LeRoy wanted to produce a re-make of *Ruggles of Red Gap* with me playing the Charles Laughton role. He even went to the trouble of hiring the original picture for me to watch. His office was in one of the bungalows on the studio lot and as I was drinking a cup of tea he had provided before viewing the film, Cary Grant entered the room. He had seen me in *Humpty Dumpty* at the Palladium in 1959 and, hearing that I was visiting Mervyn LeRoy, he had come over specially to say hello.

I was flattered by all this attention, but by this time I'd been in show business long enough to know that Robbie Burns was right when he wrote 'the best laid schemes of mice and men gang aft agley'. And so it was with *Ruggles of Red*

Gap. Correspondence went to and fro for some time, then gradually ceased. But it made me feel marvellous at the time.

The *Pickwick* company left Los Angeles as the Watts riots were beginning, and we could see the fires burning as we took off from the airport. It was a sad time to be leaving and it brought home to me the great divide that exists in American society.

Our next port of call, Cleveland, was memorable for a couple of events. The first occurred when we discovered after our Sunday off that the machinery which provided the ice for the rink in the skating scene had failed and we were ankle-deep in water when we reported for the show on the Monday.

The second event I remember was that our eldest son, Andrew, finally learned how to swim in the pool of the hotel we were staying in on Euclid Avenue.

The show received good notices, including one in the *Cleveland Plain Dealer* which referred to me as 'the nearest thing to Ionescu's bald soprano' that the reviewer had ever heard. Meanwhile we continued to rehearse extra scenes which were all eventually thrown out. One of them had a memorable lyric, 'You'll always find a chap who'll slap your back and slip you ten.' Very Dickensian, that.

Detroit was our next stop. What can I say about the city except that it was hot and humid and that Myra was refused entry to a restaurant because she was wearing a trouser suit? But this was where Roy Castle joined us with his lovely wife Fiona. It was great to have him playing Sam Weller in the show, although we were all sorry to say goodbye to Davy Jones. He went on to fame and fortune as a member of The Monkees pop group.

Detroit was not the greatest place to be staying at that time. There was growing unrest in the city and many muggings. Our stage manager was attacked and robbed under the canopy of his hotel, and our hotel receptionist used to take a taxi home every night – even though she only lived two blocks away. I had a cousin, Margaret, who, during the war, had married a Canadian airman and emigrated to toronto, so Myra and the children spent a couple of weeks with her and at weekends I would drive over the border to see them – which made a welcome change.

Washington, our next venue, was something of a contrast with elegant architecture and interesting historic sites and monuments to visit. At first we rented an apartment in the district of Alexandria – but after Jennifer and Andrew returned home to school we moved out to stay in a picturesque log cabin in the Shenandoah National Park. It meant a journey of about eighty miles each way to and from the theatre, but the air was so pure and the scenery so beautiful that the travelling was well worth the effort.

Pickwick was a critical success in Washington, and with Broadway as our next stop we all felt that the show was in good shape – or as good as it would ever be after the months of touring. It was impressed on us all by Peter Coe that the audiences we were about to play to in New York were not going to be push-overs, that the audiences in the places we had already appeared were softer and not as cynical as those in the Big Apple. Peter was preparing us for the worst, but praying for the best, because there was so much at stake for everybody concerned.

There couldn't have been a more inauspicious time to première a new Broadway musical – not only was a news-paper strike underway, but also the Pope was making an official visit to New York.

The charity preview audiences were, like most of their kind, pretty subdued. They had paid a fortune for their seats so the women were determined to show off their finery and were more interested in each other's outfits than the action on stage, while their husbands, having been dragged along, were consequently rather resentful and unappreciative of the performance.

The official opening night, however, went very well, except for one mishap when a piece of scenery fell down in the middle of the ballroom sequence – luckily without hurting anybody.

We were all in a pretty high state of expectancy as we trooped along to Sardi's Restaurant for the traditional after-show party. It is a custom on Broadway for the early editions of the morning newspapers to be brought into the restaurant and the notices to be read out. Due to the strike there were only two reviews printed. One was bad and the other was good. There were cries of outrage from the cast and murmurs of sympathy from friends as they slowly drifted away into the night. I had a sick feeling in the pit of my stomach as I shook hands with a grim-faced Peter Coe before Myra and I headed back to our penthouse apartment in the Berkshire Hotel. It was now obvious to me that *Pickwick* lacked the sharp edge which the sophisticated Broadway public wanted.

I should have smelled a rat when David Merrick chose to visit the Far East with a production of *Hello Dolly* rather than stay in New York for our opening. Bernard Delfont, I believe, had a feeling after San Francisco that Broadway might be a tougher proposition. I remember him saying 'Make the most of it, Harry,' as we shook hands before he left for England.

In spite of the poor review, the business at the box-office wasn't bad at all. The trade papers always carry the returns of every Broadway show, revealing whether a production is making a profit or a loss, and at no time during our run did we ever go into the red.

However, as fate would have it, I developed mumps – of all things – which at my time of life could be rather dangerous, and was forced to take to my bed. Myra had gone back to England with David, not thinking for one moment that there was any trouble with the show. In fact, I had asked her to arrange to ship over my Rolls-Royce as I thought it would be a good publicity gimmick.

At the end of my first week off from the show, I was lying in my hotel bed watching television. Bob Kennedy had come round for the evening to keep me company. The TV picture was quite fuzzy and Bob tried to tune it in to get a better reception to no avail. 'I'll fix the blasted thing,' I said, rising painfully from my bed. The frustration of being confined to my room and being unable to visit the theatre had made me irritable. I waddled over to the set and applied my patent method of 'fixing' television sets. I kicked it.

I swear that at that very moment the screen went black and all the room lights went off. 'I've fused the bloody lights now,' I said.

Bob looked out of the window and said, quite calmly, 'You've fused New York.'

Unbeknown to us this was the beginning of the great black-out of the city. The only lights we could see from the hotel room were the headlights and tail-lights of the cars down below in the street.

My penthouse suite was right at the top of the building and it dawned on us that Bob — who had a severe limp — was going to have to climb down dozens of flights of stairs in the pitch darkness because the elevators would be out of order. A bellboy arrived with some candles and we set about looking for the toy space-gun that young David had left behind. The gun had a red light that went on and off when the trigger was pressed. However, if you kept your finger on the trigger, it produced a steady beam of light. The drawback was that this action also produced a loud 'Whee-whee-whee' sound. Bob's progress back to his own hotel must have been an amusing sight.

I had a little transistor radio set at my bedside so that I could listen to the BBC World Service. I switched over the

FM stations to find out what had happened to the New York power supply and heard the announcement that 'all our forces are on red alert!' and that the public was 'not to panic'. Hundreds of people all over the city were trapped in lifts. It was quite gripping to lie there listening to the drama unfolding and I stopped feeling sorry for myself. 'At least,' I thought, 'there'll be no performance tonight.'

The next day when my doctor arrived to see me, the electricity supply had been restored, but he apologized for being late because so many of his elderly patients had suffered heart attacks from having to scale the stairs to their apartments at the top of skyscrapers. As he left, the doctor gave me his newspaper which I fell upon greedily. I wanted to read all the news about the black-out, but first I turned to the page containing the theatre advertisements. And there I read the customary little box with the heading '46th Street Theatre – *Pickwick*'. Underneath, below the press quote 'Should run for years', was the announcement 'Last two weeks'.

I couldn't believe it. I rang Bob immediately and asked him if what I had read was true. He had no idea and said he would ring Biff Liff, the company manager. Biff, an affable man who was genuinely fond of the show and its company, had to admit that *Pickwick* was coming off. No reason was forthcoming except that David Merrick didn't want to lose any money.

That was enough for me. I crawled out of bed and got dressed. I rang Bob again and told him that even if my wedding tackle was to hit the ground I was going back into the production to finish the last two weeks on Broadway.

I was welcomed back by the cast and by my understudy – a man even bigger than me who had found my costume too tight and 'If I Ruled the World' too high. During my absence the whole company had demanded to have innoculations against the mumps virus, a precaution that had proved very costly for Mr Merrick.

On the Tuesday of the final week, Bob came to my

dressing-room and said 'Before you get changed for the show, come to the front of the theatre for a minute.' I followed him, a bit annoyed to have my quiet time before the show interrupted. But there, in the rain, surrounded by a knot of admiring passers-by, was my grand old Rolls-Royce Silver Cloud, gleaming and fresh from its trans-Atlantic journey.

I had a lump in my throat as I patted its bonnet. 'At least we can fly the flag for the old country before we go back,' I said to Bob. And for the last few days I drove around New York in style, before watching the Rolls being loaded back on board ship for its return journey home.

The Saturday night that *Pickwick* closed found the stage door besieged by people demanding to know why such a good musical was coming off and the theatre was packed for both performances. It was a great way to finish, but I was heartbroken that all the hard work that the talented cast had put in over the months we had toured across the country had not achieved the end result we had all desired – a Broadway triumph.

And yet it was not a complete disaster, because, apart from all the money the show had made on tour – which was considerable – there was to be a pleasant postscript the following year when the Tony nominations (the Broadway equivalent of Hollywood's Oscars) were announced.

By that time *Pickwick* was long gone from Broadway and I was back in the number one dressing-room at the London Palladium. Jimmy Grafton came backstage to tell me that both Roy Castle and I had been nominated for awards for the best lead and best supporting actor in a musical respectively. Charlotte had also received a nomination for best supporting actress. There were only four nominations in each category, and although none of us was awarded the final accolade, it was a pretty good effort when one considers how very many shows come and go on Broadway in a year.

*

Four years after *Pickwick*, it was with high hopes and the same production team that the musical version of *The Four Musketeers* began to take shape. Peter Coe was to direct, Sean Kenny was the set designer and Bernard Delfont was producing. The music was by Laurie Johnson and the lyrics by Herbie Kretzmer.

When rehearsals began, Myra was expecting Katy and it was a toss up as to which production would happen first. *The Four Musketeers* won by seven days when it opened on 5 December 1967, and our lovely daughter arrived on the twelfth.

A lot of money was spent on the elaborate sets and, for the first time since the war, full use was made of the vast area of the Drury Lane stage, with all the huge stage machinery that in the past had made possible such spectacular scenes as a boat race, an avalanche, a snow storm, even an earthquake.

The costumes – which were truly magnificent – were designed by Loudon Sainthill and the cast that Peter Coe assembled promised well.

Kenneth Connor played the King; Aubrey Woods was the Cardinal; Joyce Blackham was to play Milady Clara, but did not eventually get around to doing so, and her place was taken at short notice by Elizabeth Larner; Stephanie Voss was Constance, my girlfriend; Porthos, Aramis and Athos were played by Jeremy Lloyd, John Junkin and Glyn Owen respectively, though they gave a month's notice in before the show actually opened; Jan Brinker, who was to be the Queen, also left before opening night and was replaced by Sheena Marsh; Sidney Tafler was supposed to play the Sergeant-at-Arms, but he took sick and Bill Owen took over the part. He also left the show.

As you can imagine, all this to-ing and fro-ing caused a constant draught across the stage as different members of the cast exited through the stage door. Bernie Delfont became so alarmed at what was happening that he decided to take over some of the directing himself, believing that Peter Coe had somehow lost his celebrated gift of finding the perfect cast.

I had my own problems. I had just returned from a trip to Aden for the army and, as a result of singing in the open air three or four times a day, the searing heat had damaged my vocal chords. As a precaution I pre-recorded the two big numbers in the show – 'A Little Bit of Glory' and 'The Masquerade' – with just a piano accompaniment, so that if my voice was seriously affected, I could mime to the track while the orchestra played live. Also, because Joyce Blackham had to pull out, I had very little time to rehearse with the lovely Liz Larner, and, indeed, on the first night I spent our scenes together gently guiding her to her positions on stage. I have to say that she gave a fantastic performance in spite of everything. Stephanie Voss also gave me a lot of support that night.

The massive sets presented many problems for the cast. They consisted of a complex central revolve which included four sets of stairs, each of which swivelled, integrated with great blocks, slabs and towering shapes, plus two side units that could move out on five horizontal tracks to link up to the central unit by means of flying drawbridges. In addition, there were other large units that were let down from the flies. These included arches, columns and heraldic emblems – one of which clobbered me one night. All this mechanical wizardry was worked electronically and moved while supporting members of the cast.

I remember at one dress rehearsal when, every time I was about to sing, the stairs I was standing on began to go into reverse. 'You don't want an actor!' I cried to the unfeeling moguls in the stalls. 'You want a bleeding singing goat!'

The two people responsible for setting everything in motion were the stage manager, Peter Roberts, and his very young assistant, Stella Richards. Stella was so competent at her very complex job that when the show finished I employed her as my secretary — and she was great at that job, too.

One further complication as far as I was concerned was the fact that I had to make my first act finale entrance on a horse. Now, I am not a very competent rider, and the nag I was given to ride stood nearly eighteen hands. He knew from the moment he saw me that 'here was a berk', and he devised all sorts of ways to unseat me at rehearsals. It was not until I found out from his trainer that he loved carrots that I began to make friends with him. Every performance, before I got on board the beast, I would feed him a couple of juicy carrots and on we would trot. Once, because I had run out of carrots, I gave him an apple, and he flew on stage, practically stood on his hind legs and deposited a message to me at the feet of Kenneth Connor — who was not too pleased. From then on, my dresser arranged for a constant supply of carrots with a bloke who worked at Covent Garden Market.

For the most part, the critics were not very kind about the show, but in spite of the notices, *The Four Musketeers* ran for about fourteen months. After a while, it began to get a cult following, partly because I decided that the only way to get the show going was to be even more outrageous than ever.

One night my voice was so bad that it was decided that I would have to use the tape that I had pre-recorded. I said that we should let the audience know what had happened and tell them that I would be miming to the big numbers in the show by making an announcement to that effect, and George Hoare, the manager of Drury Lane, was elected to make the announcement. The first time he did it, George was a little nervous because, when he came on, there was a murmuring from the audience as if they were expecting calamitous news. When he said I was indisposed there was quite an angry reaction, but the fact that I would be appearing, albeit hoarse, seemed to satisfy them.

When it came time for me to mime the big song 'The Masquerade', I started off perfectly seriously and in perfect synchronization with the tape. Suddenly, the bizarre nature of what I was doing got the better of me and I began to stuff a handkerchief in my mouth as my recorded voice went on. then I took a glass of water – specially set out in case I needed it to soothe my throat – and drank it slowly as the song progressed. By this time the audience, bless them, were in convulsions and at the end of the song I had more applause than I had ever had when I sang it live.

After the show, I had a chat with Jimmy Grafton and Bob Kennedy, and it was agreed that I would keep it in. The show was desperately short of laughs, and what I had just done seemed to provide the answer.

So it was that from then on, throughout the production, George Hoare made his announcement before the opening. By the time the show finished, George must have made over 300 appearances. He reckoned that it must have been some kind of theatrical record.

One night Her Majesty came to see the show from the stalls and, on her way out, she remarked to George that it would be a shame when my voice came back – a back-handed compliment, but one of which I was very proud and one which served to vindicate my decision to take a chance on sending up a good song.

It's amazing how many people have come up to me since the *Musketeer* days and said, 'I was in the audience on the night you lost your voice.' And I nod and smile, and never let on that my voice came back as strong as ever two weeks after that first announcement by George Hoare – the record breaker.

The Plumber's Progress started life as *Schippel*, written before the First World War by a German playwright called Carl Sternheim, the author of *The Mask of Virtue*, a 1935

vehicle for Vivien Leigh. *Schippel* was adapted in 1974 by
C P Taylor for the Traverse Theatre Company in Edinburgh.
Set in Germany in 1913, the piece told the tale of a quartet of
class-conscious Meister Singers who, with the demise of their
tenor, are forced – against their better social instincts – to
recruit the local plumber, a gifted singer, in his place.

Jimmy Grafton saw the play and decided that it would be
perfect for me for a West End comeback. I went to see it at
the Open Space Theatre and I was captivated by the concept.

When I saw it, the leading part of the tenor, Schippel, was
played by Roy Marsden. He gave a great performance and I
felt somewhat embarrassed about taking over the role from
him. It says a lot for Roy's breadth of spirit that he stayed
with the production in a lesser part and agreed to act as my
understudy.

Bernard Delfont who had produced all my shows for as
long as I could remember, thought that it would be a good
vehicle for me at the Prince of Wales Theatre, although he
wanted to change the name. He thought *Schippel* sounded
too much like the Dutch airport and didn't want audiences to
come to the show thinking that they were going to see me
playing a singing air steward. So the title was altered to *The
Plumber's Progress*, which caused a certain amount of
controversy among the purists.

The cast was particularly strong. Priscilla Morgan (Clive
Dunn's wife) and Patricia Heneghan played the sister and
wife respectively of Tilman Hiketier, the goldsmith and leader
of the quartet, who was played by Roger Kemp. Roy
Marsden and Gordon Clyde portrayed the other members of
the singing group and Simon Callow was Crown Prince
Maximilian. The director was Mike Ockrent, who has since
made quite a name for himself in the theatre.

Mike was extremely kind to me at rehearsals, teaching me
how to control my wilder moments and how to change the
mood without jarring the whole production. I was

determined to play the part straight and not indulge myself in ad libbing, which I had been forced to do in *The Four Musketeers* out of sheer desperation. As the singing all came naturally out of the context of the play – for example when Schippel auditioned for Hiketier – I did not have the awkward transition from dialogue to song. When we sang as a quartet we were accompanied by a piano on stage played by Gordon Clyde, one of the members of the quartet.

I found the rehearsals invigorating, working as an ensemble player throughout the piece, learning how to blend with the other actors. All the music was sung in German, which could have been a bit of a turn-off for some members of the audience, but it was true to the piece.

In September 1975, we opened in Manchester for a two-week try-out at the Opera House. The play was received pretty well and took just over £7,000 for five performances in the first week. However, I sensed that there might be trouble ahead when I overheard a lady's comment as she passed under my dressing-room window after one of the performances. 'I'm not paying good money to hear Harry Secombe say "bollocks",' she said firmly.

When we opened at the Prince of Wales with a charity performance for the Variety Club of Great Britain, exception was taken to the singing of 'Deutschland Uber Alles' at the final curtain. This was deliberate – the song emphasized the resurgence of German militarism as portrayed by the fanaticism of Hiketier, the quartet's leader. It was meant to be ironic but I suppose it could have been taken the wrong way by certain sections of the audience. The decision was taken to change the final song to 'Stille Nacht', which somehow emasculated the effect that Sternheim and C P Taylor had originally desired.

The reviews after the first night were nearly all good. Sheridan Morley wrote 'the result is a broad comedy with, at its centre, the resolutely unchanging Schippel, unflinchingly working class and deaf to all entreaties to improve himself or his station. It is a comic performance I shall long treasure and I see no reason why Mr Secombe should not now start thinking about *The Good Soldier Schweik*, maybe even *Peer Gynt*.'

Michael Billington's review went 'Snobs will be upset that *The Plumber's Progress* has found its way from the Traverse Theatre Club to the Prince of Wales, but personally I'm delighted to see the commanding heights of the West End falling one by one to the subsidized companies and Mike Ockrent's production of this anti-bourgeois satire of 1912 has undergone physical expansion without sacrificing its precision.'

The Plumber's Progress was a fruitful experience as far as I was concerned because I learned so much from working with the other actors. They were all very generous to me on stage and off and I have watched the subsequent rise to fame of Simon Callow and Roy Marsden with a great deal of satisfaction. I was very upset when I had to leave the show with a viral pneumonia, and though Roy carried on for a few performances as Schippel, he developed a throat infection and the show had to come off. It was never a huge box-office success, but it was mounted at a time when all the West End theatres were suffering a listless period. Perhaps if the production had been in a smaller theatre we might have run longer, but there is no point in looking for excuses in our profession. If the public like what you have to offer they will come and see it, and if they don't, well, they won't.

There are so many excuses made for badly attended shows, but the most priceless I have ever heard was Arthur Askey's. He always used to say, 'There'll be nobody in tonight – there's pearl diving at Oldham.'

A Wanderlust

Ever since I was a small boy, I have longed to find out what lies over the next horizon. I used to sit on the front gate of our council house at 7 St Leger Crescent, St Thomas, Swansea, South Wales, Great Britain, Europe, The World, and gaze longingly in the direction of Town Hill, because my dad told me that that was where the West was and that America was over there somewhere. As far as I was concerned, buffalo roamed on the other side of that hill and you could get scalped in Llansamlet.

As I grew older, my horizons got wider and my desire to travel grew proportionately. My army service took me to North Africa, Sicily and Italy via troop ships, landing craft, bren carriers and three-ton trucks – which was not exactly the way that Thomas Cook would have planned it, but was enough to whet my appetite for further excursions, without, of course, the necessity of having to persuade the Germans in front to keep moving.

When I became more affluent, obscure places beckoned and I would set off with Myra and our two children, Jennifer and Andrew, on holiday trips to what were in those days fairly remote Caribbean islands like Trinidad and Tobago. It was an adventure to travel by plane then and we would all be togged up in brand new outfits for the journey and both sets of parents would come to the airport to see us off. Then we would pose for photographs at the foot of the airline steps before boarding the plane. The reason for this was twofold: one, to show the general public that we were brave enough to fly BOAC; two, if anything happened to the plane, Associated Press would have a scoop on their hands – 'Comedian and Family Before Fateful Flight'.

Nowadays, travel is much more sophisticated and the world has shrunk. There is even a Hilton International hotel at Llansamlet, where you won't get scalped but you might get a decent haircut.

Africa never ceased to fascinate me. As a child I was always off hunting lions or cutting my way through the dense undergrowth of our local park and when, some years later, I was invited on a safari, I was off like a shot to the Army & Navy Stores to be fitted for shorts and several pairs of unsoiled white duck.

It was thus attired that I strode out on to the verandah of my hotel in Nairobi, showing a full inch of leg between the bottom of my shorts and the tops of my khaki stockings. On my head I wore a bush hat, and a pair of suede boots completed my white hunter ensemble. Across the hotel gardens a parrot chained to a stand sent up a raucous screeching, and an American couple having an early breakfast paused abruptly in mid-kedgeree. I went back to my room and changed. If I was ready for Africa, Africa was not quite ready for me.

My spirits lightened as we headed for Nairobi National Park, where giraffe, lion and all sorts of other wild life go about their business with complete disregard for the planes roaring over their heads as they fly to and from the airport.

We had only just got inside the Park when a large baboon jumped on the bonnet and performed a disgustingly human act, after which it bowed politely and held out its hand for a nut. It was like that all the way: lions rolled playfully on their backs like cats wanting to be tickled, giraffes nibbled disdainfully at the tops of thorn bushes and ignored us completely.

Disillusionment set in. Where was my Africa? The Africa of my boyhood imaginings? This was Longleat with flies.

Our next stop was Murchison Falls and, after a dusty but fairly uneventful journey into Uganda, we arrived some days later on the banks of the White Nile just in time to catch the last ferry to the camp. During our short stay at Murchison, we were able to observe hippos and elephants without the slightest danger – a fact that began to irk me after a while. I was still in search of the real, unspoiled Africa.

My chance came a few days later when I was invited to accompany a game warden on one of his regular trips in search of poachers. Our base was a permanent camp near the Ugandan border with the Congo. We were going to sleep in sleeping bags and really rough it. At last, I thought, this is it.

On the way to the camp, I heard two of the native boys who were travelling with us referring to me several times in what I took to be Swahili. When we got there, I mentioned this to the warden.

'That's good,' he said. 'If they have a special name for you it means they respect you. Try to find out what it is.'

The camp consisted of one round metal hut with a straw roof and a wooden table. It was getting late, so the boys built a big fire and set tin plates on the table. Beer was produced and, as a Tilley lamp pumped a brilliant circle of light around the table, dinner began.

Somewhere an animal snuffled and, flushed with beer, I smiled to myself. I was Mungo Park, Livingstone and Chaka the Zulu chief all rolled into one. This was how I had always imagined it – the camp fire, the animal noises and the convivial chat around the table. Soon it will be time to slip into our sleeping bags while the native boys keep the fire going and ward off the animals, I thought.

The table was cleared and the boys, to my amazement, retired into the metal hut and shut the door.

'Time for bed,' said the warden, stretching. 'If you want to go to the toilet, there's one over there.' He pointed vaguely into the blackness. ' 'Night.'

I sat for a while drinking beer and keeping the fire going until, with the last piece of wood gone, I struggled into my sleeping bag, whistling tunelessly and staring uneasily about me. There was the whole Aardvark to Zebra of African wildlife out there, and here I was lying on the ground in this open air supermarket, two hundred and twenty pounds of human flesh, fresh and ready wrapped.

I eventually fell asleep, but dawn was never as welcome as the next morning. I was up and sluicing my naked body as the native boys emerged from the safety of their hut.

One of them laughed and pointed at me. 'Tumbo Mkubwa,' he said.

I turned proudly to the game warden who was now awake and regarding me with some amusement.

'There, that's the name they called me yesterday. What does it mean?'

He scratched his head and stretched his arms out wide, taking his time. 'Big Belly,' he said.

Somehow, it was the final indignity.

As a family we have travelled many times around the world on the way to concert tours in Australia and New Zealand, dropping off at Hong Kong or Singapore on the outward flight and Fiji or Hawaii on the return journey. The very names of these exotic places are still fascinating to me and the fact that I've had prickly heat in all of them still does not put me off. Even the fact that I have never had a suit that fitted made in twenty-four hours by a Hong Kong tailor is no deterrent to my urge to travel. Myra had one of these suits made into seat covers for her car and still had enough left over for a table cloth. The fly buttons that adorned it were always a good topic of conversation with visitors who came to tea in Cheam.

We have had a place in Majorca since 1963. Myra and I had holidayed there a couple of times previously and had taken a liking to the island. Jimmy Grafton had a villa in Paguera, which he sold in favour of an apartment in a new development called Costa de los Pinos which was on the other side of the island, and one day he suggested to me that perhaps we would like to go out there and see if we too would like to invest in property in the same complex.

It didn't take us long to decide that we would indeed fancy one of the houses there. We chose one on the hillside on which the collection of villas and apartments had been built, a promontory jutting out into the sea and forming the north end of a beautiful bay encompassing miles of golden sand.

I was still doing *Pickwick* at the Saville Theatre when we moved into the villa, and it provided the perfect bolt-hole for the family. In the summer, Myra would go over with her parents and Andrew, Jennifer and David, who was then still a babe in arms. I would join them at weekends, catching a late-night flight from Gatwick – usually by the skin of my teeth – and returning on the Monday morning plane from Palma. It might seem like a lot of trouble for twenty-four hours in the sun, but to me it was well worth the effort. To be able to enjoy the view from our balcony and smell the pine-scented air more than compensated for the time taken up by travelling.

The nearby village of Son Servera was where we did our shopping and the locals soon got used to the fat foreigner with the pretty little dark wife – who they all thought was

Spanish. My knowledge of Spanish was very rudimentary and I soon became a source of entertainment for the customers at the butcher's shop as I had to order what I wanted in mime. For example, for a shoulder of lamb, I would pat my own shoulder and bleat baa-baa. For a leg of the same animal I would, obviously, indicate my leg. A chicken was dead easy as I've always been able to cluck. A rump steak was always a tap on the behind accompanied by a mooing sound. I never really got around to ordering sausages.

As the years went by and Katy came along and the other three got bigger, the little villa seemed to shrink in size. Myra was finding the place a bit claustrophobic and the journey she had to make down to the little cove below us and back again up the many steep steps to the house, which happened about three times a day, was beginning to get her down. So it was either sell up and leave Majorca, or find another place not too far away.

Jimmy Grafton came to the rescue. He had seen a villa for sale about a mile down the coast, right on the sea. It was newly built and could be exactly what we wanted. He was dead right, as usual, and the whole family fell in love with it. The entrance to the house was through an archway into a little courtyard, where an ornamental fountain played away. Inside, there were two bedrooms on the ground floor with toilets and bathrooms en suite, and a large dining and living room combined, while upstairs there was a master bedroom with French windows that led on to a patio facing the sea, with stunning views of the pine-clad hills of Costa de los Pinos on our left and the sea at our back garden gate.

I was in Australia at the time, and Myra moved in as soon as she was able without telling me. After the long journey back to Palma via Los Angeles, New York and Madrid, I was met at the airport by Myra and Jennifer. Feeling pretty jet-lagged, after the excitement of seeing the family again, all

I wanted was to get into bed. But, as we headed for where I thought we still lived, Myra insisted that we paid a visit to the new villa so that I could see how it was getting on. 'Can't I see it later?' I yawned, desperate for a kip. Of course, when we turned into the new address, the rest of the family were all waiting to welcome me. It was a wonderful surprise and my tiredness vanished immediately, only to return hours later when my head fell in the gazpacho at dinner.

'Don't worry,' said Myra. 'It was cold anyway.'

That was twenty-two years ago and we're still in love with the place. In recent years, Majorca has suffered from the bad reputation it has received from reports in the tabloid press about the behaviour of 'lager louts' in the fleshpots of Arenal and Magaluf. But there are still little-known corners of the island where the tourist in search of beautiful scenery allied with peace and tranquillity can find what he is looking for: where honeysuckle grows in profusion and blackberries ripen unseen; where eagles ride the thermals above rock-clad mountain peaks and shepherds tend flocks of wiry sheep whilst listening to their personal stereos. Well, you can't get away from everything.

It was only when we had been living there for about ten years that we began to understand the Majorcan people and the workings of the Majorcan mind. Shopkeepers will say yes out of politeness. We had half an iron gate for four years, and it was considerably longer before we could get rid of the string that held the shutters open. Every six months the local blacksmith calls around for a sherry and a look at the jobs he hasn't yet finished. He nods, promises, asks after the family, then we ask after his and that's it for another six months.

We had a hole in the ground for two years before it underwent its metamorphosis into a swimming pool. Strange-looking weeds grew out of it, the kids kept falling into it and every time we came out for a holiday we went through the ritual of pleas and promises with the builder.

Then, suddenly one Easter, it was practically finished . . . and it stayed practically finished until we went back in August.

Majorcans have a very keen sense of humour, which they conceal beneath an outward appearance of dourness. When I went to pay the plumber's bill one day in Son Servera, his wife searched through the files for it to no avail. I repeated my name with the Spanish pronunciation I had become used to – (SEC-OM-BEE) – but she still couldn't find it. Then her husband came in and took over the search. He found it easily, and when I asked him why his wife had been unable to do so, he grinned and showed me the name under which it had been filed: 'El Gordo' – 'The Fat One'. Later on, I discovered that I was also known as 'El Tenor' (The Tenor) or 'El Cantante' (The Singer). This came about because, in a rash moment, I gave a café owner one of my records. It was a mistake because for weeks after, whenever I entered his café he put the damned thing on at full volume. He seemed to think that that was the reason I had given it to him – I had it on authority that it was never played at any other time. There's only so much of my own voice that I can stand listening to and in the end I had to plead with him not to play the record. He agreed reluctantly, or so it seemed until out of the corner of my eye I caught him winking at his waiter. There is subtlety in abundance in the Majorcan character.

Majorca is my second home, but if I could afford a *third* house it would definitely be in Australia. I love the place.

The first time I went there was in 1961 when I was booked to appear in a television show and a concert in the Sydney Town Hall. I was enchanted by the place and the people and for the first time I began to realize how popular the *Goon Show* had become outside the UK. I was constantly being greeted by cries of 'Hello Ned,' or 'How's Eccles?' by people in the street. The programmes had been going out on ABC Radio for some time and had become something of a cult.

I did not exactly take the place by storm, but I was sufficiently taken by my reception to want to return there as soon as I was able. However, it was not until 1969 that I was free to make another trip to Australia. This time I was booked to appear for four weeks at St George's Club in Sydney. This was a huge Taj Mahal-type building run by the Returned Servicemen's League. Inside there was every type of gambling including a host of one-armed bandit machines from which came most of the club's revenue.

It was a time when many English and American artists were looking for new venues to play outside their own countries. For some who were well past their sell-by dates, Australia was a welcome source of income although they could be given a hard time by club audiences if their acts were not up to scratch. Having been disillusioned by a succession of self-proclaimed Las Vegas or Palladium 'top-liners', I found the audiences were determined to assess the worth of my performance for themselves and one had to earn their approval. They were not prepared to give a big hand when the act was introduced, but if they liked what they saw, they were unstinting in their applause at the end. So I was pleasantly surprised on the Saturday night of my first week at St George's, to receive a standing ovation – my first ever. My first thought was that it might be mass cramp considering the age of some members of the audience, but it was for real and my heart leaped. Of course there were many ex-pats out front who had come to cheer, but there were plenty of home-grown Aussies too and from them it was a genuine seal of approval.

I have been back many times over the years – sometimes twice a year – and I have travelled all over that continent and both North and South Islands of New Zealand. There was one memorable show in Kalgoorlie that sticks in my mind. I flew in on a private jet along with Jimmy Grafton and Bob Kennedy to be met by a civic reception. At the time I was wearing a blue and white striped blazer prompting the mayor to remark, somewhat acidly, that if he had known I was going to be wearing a butcher's apron he would not have bothered to put on his chain of office.

The concert was held in a football stadium on a specially built stage and the promoter had borrowed a brand new baby grand piano from the mayor's parlour. Kalgoorlie is a gold-mining town in the heart of the desert and, at the time of my arrival, had been without rain for many months.

The show had only been going for about twenty minutes when the previously starry night sky began to cloud over and ominous distant rumbles of thunder were heard.

'Don't worry, Harry,' said the promoter. 'It never rains here.'

A few minutes later, just as I had started to sing 'Bless This House', lightning flashed and the heavens opened. As the rain poured down, the audience rose to its feet and cheered – not me but the rain. The shower lasted long enough to ruin the mayor's piano and my dinner suit but there were no complaints from a soaking wet public. 'Good on yer, mate!' was the cry as I paddled damply off stage and for the rest of the tour I was known as the 'Rain Maker'.

At the beginning of the 1970s, Stan Mars, an associate of Jimmy Grafton's, was inspired to write the screenplay for a film based on a poster he had seen advertising for teachers in Australia. The poster had depicted a schoolmaster in mortar board and gown and wearing a pair of shorts, posing in brilliant sunshine on Bondi Beach, and thus the film *Sunstruck* was born.

The story was about a middle-aged school teacher in South Wales who, having been rejected by his girlfriend, sees the poster and decides to emigrate to Australia. He fancies himself as a sun-tanned figure standing on the golden sands of a spectacular beach under a cloudless blue sky, living an idyllic life in some fancy Sydney suburb.

Instead, he finds himself in the outback, miles from the sea and having to teach a bunch of recalcitrant youngsters who live in a small farming community. He gets into all sort of trouble as he tries to fit in with the locals and falls out with the landlord of the only pub in the area, played by that fine actor John Meillon. Eventually, he wins over the community and forms a school choir which goes to Sydney and is successful in a choral competition. Along the way he becomes romantically involved with a lady played by Maggie Fitzgibbon, who runs a farm and, of course, it all ends happily. A slight story indeed.

James Gilbert, an old friend from BBC Television, directed the film, which incidentally was the only one being made in Australia at that time. Impresario Jack Neary, who had originally brought me out to Sydney, was executive producer along with Jimmy Grafton. The first scenes, showing the school in South Wales, had to be shot in the worst possible weather so that it would be a tremendous contrast to the brilliance of Bondi Beach – but things did not work out too well to begin with. The location of the school was set in Treharris, where my mother was born, and Donald Houston took the part of the sports master who was my rival for the affection of the girl teacher we both fancied.

It seemed that everybody in the town had known my mother and I was constantly being introduced to aunts and uncles and distant cousins. I was awash with tea and Welsh cakes. The attention I was attracting did not interfere with the filming because we were waiting for the bright sunlight overhead to change to the overcast sky we wanted for the contrast with Bondi Beach. I was having a great time meeting my long-lost relations but poor old Jimmy Gilbert was getting desperate about going over budget as we waited for rain. In the end we got what we wanted and it was 'Australia here we come'. When we turned up at Bondi about a week later, it was overcast and raining and we had to wait a day or two before we could get those sparkling sunlit shots we needed. I got the feeling somebody was trying to tell us something.

The main location for the shooting was a place called Parkes in Western New South Wales and the film unit took over the whole of a motel outside the town. It was a typical little outback community consisting of one main street in which verandahed shops sold agricultural implements, clothing and fast food and in every one we entered we were asked if we were the film people. We caused quite a stir amongst the very hospitable citizens.

The family had all come out to join me. Jennifer was working as an assistant publicity officer for the film company, and David and Katy, because they were away from school, had to have private tuition while we were filming.

The heat was quite like that which I had experienced in North Africa, dry and dusty, and it took some getting used to. As we drove the long journey from Sydney to Parkes, Myra and Jennifer began to have grave doubts about the smart evening wear they had brought with them for cocktail and dinner parties. 'I think we'll have to settle for a couple of sheep-shearers' vests,' said Myra as the dusty road unwound before us. As it turned out, after a couple of days' filming, the ladies of the unit began to make an effort to dress up for the evening meal and my two soon joined in. One member of the cast, Norman Erskine, a very large tough-looking actor with a wry sense of humour was moved to say to Myra, 'For an old Sheila you don't look too bad.'

The one big problems about filming was the presence of the flies. They were not like our English ones who have the decency to fly off after being swatted away – these Aussie ones kept coming back, clinging to the corners of one's eyes and mouth with great tenacity. They can also bite. Much time was wasted trying to get 'flyless shots', especially close-ups. One way to keep them at bay was to use a fly spray but sometimes it could cause a sneezing bout amongst actors and crew, and filming would be held up even longer. When the refreshment van drove up to the location you could follow its progress on the horizon by the swarm of accompanying winged insects. When the van finally arrived it was a battle to get a mouthful of tea before the flies got to it. 'Every biscuit a Garibaldi' as Norman Erskine remarked, removing a couple of the cursed creatures from his tongue. We all developed what is called Down Under the 'Bush Salute' – a waving motion of the hand before the face which became automatic as soon as we left the cool sanctuary of our hotel for the heat of the day.

Another thing to worry about was the snake population. When the prop men were renovating an old tumbledown house to turn it into a pub, four brown snakes fell on them from the rafters above. When it came time for me to do my scenes in there I made sure that I was word-perfect because I had no intention of hanging about. Night filming was also hazardous. The moment that the powerful lights were switched on, every living, flying creature for miles around descended on us. Kamikaze beetles threw themselves at the lamps and huge moths flew sorties in the arc light's beam only to sizzle bravely as they hit their target. We managed to complete the filming by the miracle of Jimmy Gilbert's patience and the complete dedication of cast and crew. In spite of all the trouble, everyone seemed to enjoy themselves. As a family we had a great time and David and Katy came away having learned an entirely new vocabulary of quaint Australian expressions from the crew – some of which upset their teachers when they got back to school.

Sunstruck was the last family film to be made in Australia before a flood of productions of a more adult nature overtook it, and I'm afraid it sank almost without trace. It was a pity really because there were some good performances from Maggie Fitzgibbon and John Meillon, and Jimmy Gilbert did an excellent job as director. It can be found occasionally in the early dawn programmes for insomniacs, but it's still good for a chuckle or two. Incidentally, Hal McElroy, who was on the production side, went on with his brother to produce the acclaimed *Picnic at Hanging Rock*.

One traumatic incident in my life that I will always associate with Australia – even though it only really started there – was the first time I had been seriously ill since childhood.

It was late 1980, about halfway through the last week of my Australian tour. I was performing at the Twin Towns RSL Club, right on the border between New South Wales and Queensland. As a matter of fact, the hotel I was staying at was in Queensland and the club, just across the road, was in New South Wales.

A niggly pain started low down in my left side, and because I knew that appendicitis affected the right side, I put it down to indigestion – and, anyway, I was going to Barbados to join Myra and the kids for Christmas. *Nothing* was going to stop me from getting on that plane.

When I woke up on the Sunday morning the pain had got worse and I had a terrible headache which no aspirin could touch. Dennis Smith, my Australian agent and a very good friend, was most concerned. 'Are you sure you can make the journey?' he asked, going on to outline the route. 'You've got to go on your own from the airport here at Surfer's Paradise to Sydney, wait three hours, then on to Los Angeles via Honolulu. There's a five hour wait in Los Angeles where you have to change planes. Then it's on to New York for another five hour wait and another change of planes to Barbados. You don't look as if you can make it up the road to Coolangatta, let alone fly all those miles to Barbados, mate.'

I convinced him that it was a recurrence of some old stomach trouble and that I would be OK.

The journey was a nightmare. The flight attendants wanted to put me off the plane in Hawaii, but I insisted it was a touch of flu. By the time I got to Los Angeles I was hallucinating. I sat in the terminal for four hours and witnessed all sorts of weird happenings. Mind you, Los Angeles Airport lounges can be like that at the best of times. I managed to make the change of planes and was again questioned about my health, but my determination to get to Barbados and my waiting family helped me to persuade the purser that I just had an upset stomach. All the time I was airborne I was unable to eat – all I could do was drink soda water.

The change of planes at New York was the worst. It was snowing and I was only wearing a blazer and flannels. I didn't realize that I had to go to another terminal which entailed getting on to a bus outside the airport with all my luggage.

I am not going to pile on the agony, but to cut a long story short, I eventually landed in Barbados on the Monday afternoon. Myra, David and Katy were in the reception area at the airport. They waved to me through the glass and I put on a big grin and waved back. 'Be right with you,' I mouthed, not knowing that my luggage – which had travelled all the way from Surfer's Paradise – had been left behind in New York. After reporting the loss to officials and filling in forms, it was another hour before I was at last reunited with my family.

I managed to play down my pain all that afternoon and evening, until at about two o'clock in the morning it got the better of me. Myra managed to get a doctor on the phone but when she had described my symptoms to him he sleepily declared that he was on the other side of the island and that anyway it sounded like colic to him. 'Give him a couple of aspirins,' he said. 'I'll see him in the morning.'

The pain became more intense and by the time he eventually turned up to see me I felt pretty rough. 'My word, you're in a bad state,' was his first bright remark. 'I'll come and see you again this afternoon,' he said after a somewhat perfunctory examination. He handed some tablets to Myra and went off to play golf.

A couple of hours later he was prised away from the golf course by a frantic call from Myra. This time he could see that I was in desperate trouble. He sent for an ambulance and after a rocky ride I arrived at the Queen Elizabeth Hospital in Bridgetown. The attendants put my stretcher down on the floor at reception while the necessary paperwork was transacted. 'Oh look!' said a couple of passing tourists. 'It's Harry Secombe.' And so strong is the 'ham' in me that I managed a deprecating grin and a wiggle of the fingers.

I was now safely in the hands of a very competent medical staff who soon whipped me into a ward where I was examined by Mr Irving Smith, a Barbadian surgeon who had been a lecturer in surgery at Edinburgh University. He immediately sent me to the x-ray department and when he had seen the results he said, 'I'm afraid I've got to go in there.' He sounded a bit like the US Fifth Cavalry. 'It looks very nasty,' he said to Myra. 'I think he's got peritonitis.'

She turned to David and said, 'That's what his sister Joan died of.'

One thought flashed into my mind as I lay on the stretcher. A couple of years before, Arthur Dickson Wright, a famous surgeon and wit, had told me that if he had to operate on me he would wear bathing trunks and a pair of Wellingtons and open me up with a six-foot scalpel.

I don't remember much about what happened next, except the pain and saying to a gowned operation theatre assistant, 'I've played many theatres in my life, but this is the first Operating Theatre.' Not very witty, but apposite, I thought, before going to sleep.

I woke up about six hours later in the recovery room, to

find that I had all sorts of tubes poking out of various parts of my anatomy, and that the intolerable pain had been reduced to a dull throb. 'At least I'm alive,' I thought and went back to sleep.

When I came to again a tearful Myra and a very serious David were at my bedside. 'The surgeon told me you only had a fifty-fifty chance of coming out of the operation the right side up,' she said, squeezing my hand. 'You had a perforated colon.'

I tried to make a joke about suffering from 'punctuation', but the tube up my nose spoiled my delivery. David smiled anyway.

Irving Smith came to see how I was feeling. I thanked him profusely for saving my life. 'Don't thank me,' he said. 'Thank Him.' And he pointed his finger heavenwards.

He told me that he had also removed my appendix – as an encore I suppose – and that a blood test before the actual operation had revealed that I was suffering from diabetes. 'Nothing to worry about as long as you look after yourself,' he said with a smile and a parting wave of the hand.

The nurses were great to me – especially one very large lady who was as strong as an ox. She used to lift me up on her own while another nurse straightened the sheet beneath me, and would let me down as lightly as a feather.

I'll never forget one Sunday morning, just before Christmas Day, when an old ward maid came in at about five o'clock to open the windows wider and tidy up the ward.

I was feeling particularly sorry for myself that morning. The stitches were beginning to hurt, my backside was numb and I had a thumping headache. Not even the sounds of a Barbadian early morning – the cooing of the pigeons and the first throaty cock crows – or the perfume of the frangipani and hibiscus outside the window could lift my spirits.

The old lady, sensing my mood, came and stood beside my

bed. She had no idea who I was – just some poor soul in pain. She gave me a lovely smile and, holding my hand, she said a little prayer for me. Then she went on her way.

From then on I began to feel better.

Convalescence was slow, partly because my diabetic condition slowed down the healing process, although I could not have been in a better place in which to get well. The after-care at the Queen Elizabeth Hospital was excellent, but I was anxious to get back to the hotel with Myra and the kids. They had to take a taxi across the island to see me every day and, naturally, the Christmas festivities were spoiled for them. So it was a great relief when I was allowed out of hospital for New Year's Eve.

Budge and Cynthia O'Hara who ran the Settlers Beach Hotel have been friends of ours for many years. They treated Myra and myself like royalty, and the house we were staying in was always full of fruit and flowers.

Day by day I took longer walks along the sands with Myra steadying me until I was able to toddle along unaided. Together we would sit on the beach and watch for the green flash which was said to come just the second before the sun went down into the sea. We never actually saw it, but it was fun looking for it.

I was very moved by the letters and phone messages wishing me well. Danny La Rue, God bless him, rang from Australia to enquire about me and I had a cable from Spike and Peter which read 'Get a second opinion from a witch doctor.'

As I said, this was the first time that I had been seriously ill since I was a child, and as I lay in bed I began to come to terms with the fact that I would have to start taking care of myself. I remember looking at my arms and thinking 'These are an old man's arms.' They were flaccid and wrinkled, not plump and firm as they once were. I realized they hadn't got that way overnight, the process had begun gradually, but I was not in the habit of checking myself out for signs of old age. Now, lying around with nothing to do, I was able to take stock of myself. My girth was considerably reduced as an effect of the operation and the scar which ran from my navel downwards was not a pretty sight, but the rest of me could do with an overhaul. The diabetes would have to be controlled for a start, and Myra had a look in her eye that said that I would diet whether I liked it or not. And so I did, at least for a while.

My principal worry was that the operation might have weakened the muscles around the diaphragm, making singing more difficult. I could still do comedy, but without the odd song or two my act would be a bit weak. Man cannot live on raspberries alone. Another worry was the fact that I was very constipated and I was afraid of the stitches bursting if I tried to relieve myself. I toyed with the idea of singing a couple of notes to see if everything was all right down there, but kept saying to myself 'Have a go tomorrow.' Eventually I managed to summon up the courage when I was in the toilet to let rip with a couple of top Cs. People ran from all over Settlers Beach to find out where the loud sound was coming from.

Myra was the first one into the house. She had been on the beach sunbathing at the time. She burst into the loo to discover me with my trousers around my ankles and a beatific smile on my face.

'I can do it!' I cried. 'I can do it!'

'I can see that,' she said. 'But what was all the noise about?'

Fortunately I had taken out an insurance policy before I left for the tour because I had to stay on at the hotel in Barbados for another four weeks before I was allowed to fly home. I needed all that time to get my strength back.

While we were waiting for the plane to take us home, a lady approached Myra and asked 'What's the matter with the old man?' That set me firmly on the way back to recovery. After all, I was only fifty-nine.

During my early visits to Australia it was interesting to see how the building of the new Opera House in Sydney Harbour was progressing. Opinions about its design were mixed and the architects came in for some heavy criticism from the national press. Some said that it looked as if it had been doodled on the back of an old envelope.

To my untutored eye I thought it looked very impressive and added to the beauty of the harbour, so when I was invited to perform in the inaugural concert on the day after its ceremonial opening by the Queen, I was extremely flattered and even muted my raspberry blowing in deference to the occasion.

It was generally accepted that of the two main theatres which comprised the Opera House, the one which was supposed to be for operatic productions did not have an orchestra pit big enough to contain the musicians required for grand opera performances, while the other hall, designed for concert performances, *did* have enough space for a large orchestra. So the opera theatre became the concert hall, and vice versa. Anyway, it was a great thrill to be performing in such pristine conditions, although there was some trouble with the sound system to start with.

I have played there many times since, but one particular concert sticks out in my memory. It was a year after my operation and although I knew that I was diabetic I was not really taking my condition seriously. I had been performing once again at the Twin Towns RSL Club, for a week before coming down to Sydney for the Opera House show. At that time I was still much heavier than was healthy for me, about seventeen and a half stone, and I had not given up drinking.

It was a special concert that Dennis Smith had arranged:

the Sydney Welsh male voice choir – about 100 of them – was backing me and I was accompanied by the Australian pop orchestra which consisted of sixty-odd musicians. Normally on such occasions with such magnificent support I came off stage on a high, but this particular night, even though the audience gave me a standing ovation, it was all I could do to walk off to my dressing-room where I lay down on a settee. All around me my usual Aussie mates Billy Rowe, my road manager, Peter Worram, my accompanist, and Dennis Smith, along with Jimmy Grafton, were bustling about dispensing drinks to the management and other members of the cast, while Myra, who could see that I was in a bad way, sat alongside me on the settee holding my hand. She called Dennis over and said 'Harry's not at all well. He said he nearly passed out on stage.'

I didn't want any fuss that night but agreed to see a doctor the following morning in his surgery in the Rocks area. When I turned up there I was accompanied by a whole retinue of concerned people: Dennis, Billy, Jimmy, Peter and of course Myra. The doctor was a large burly Greek Australian called Nick Paphos, to whom Dennis took any of his artistes who were taken ill. 'Which one of you is the patient?' he said, winking at me. I gave him a sickly grin because I was not in the mood for jokes, and he waved the others into his waiting room, taking just Myra and me into his surgery.

He gave me a thorough examination, even the dreaded prostate exploration. My voice went up an octave at the sight of the rubber glove, and my strained attempts at casual conversation from the very undignified position in which he placed me, set Myra giggling. 'Lovely place to sing in the OPERA HOUSE!!' was the observation I made which nearly sent my wife into hysterics. After he had finished probing and prodding and paying the Barbadian surgeon's work a nice compliment, he told me to get dressed. Then he sat down at his desk and wrote down some notes on his pad, which Myra, sitting opposite, tried to read upside down.

When I was finished dressing, he addressed me very seriously. 'Harry, your blood sugar level is sky high, your blood pressure is through the roof, you've got an infected throat, and to top it all, mate, you're five stone too heavy. I'll give you two years at the most if you don't look after yourself. Go on a diet, cut out the booze, and you've got a chance.' He turned to Myra, 'You'd better make sure that he looks after himself.'

'Don't worry,' she said very firmly. 'I'll see that he does.'

And believe me, she did. From then on, I was on a strict diet and from that day to this, I have never touched a drop of alcohol. I needed his straight talking and Myra's determination to make sure that I followed his instructions, to jolt me into the realization that I was in mortal danger if I didn't change my eating and drinking habits. In a way, Nick Paphos saved my life and I shall be eternally grateful to him.

Several years later I received a newspaper cutting in a letter from Dennis Smith. It was from a Sydney paper and told of Nick Paphos being jailed for drug smuggling. Apparently he and a couple of others had purchased an old tramp steamer in Piraeus harbour, loaded it with cannabis and had a crew sail it to a point off Darwin on the North Australian coast. It was unloaded into small boats and the cargo brought ashore. The crew was paid off and the ship scuttled. The cannabis was then transported in lorries from Darwin down to Sydney. However, the authorities had been tipped off and the cargo came under police surveillance from the moment it left Darwin. Nick and his accomplices were arrested red-handed with the drugs in Sydney and were all sent down for several years apiece.

He was a fine doctor and now that he has paid his debt to society, I hope he has been accepted back into the mainstream of life and found happiness. I wrote to him several times when he was in prison but had no reply. Perhaps one day we'll meet up again and I can thank him for what he did for me.

It is said that everyone remembers where they were when President Kennedy was assassinated and when John Lennon was shot. I was making up as Samuel Pickwick in my dressing-room at the Saville Theatre when Kennedy was killed and I heard the news about John Lennon in my room on the leisure complex on Lizard Island on the Great Barrier Reef off Cairns in Northern Queensland. It was my third visit to the island having first set foot there when it was completely undeveloped except for a rough landing strip, a tractor and a wooden toilet. We had flown in as a family by courtesy of Syd Williams, the chairman of Bush Pilot Airways, who we had met at a hotel in Cairns. It turned out that he and his wife had been hosts to Prince Charles when he had been on holiday from his boarding school.

We told them that we were going on to Dunk Island for a holiday and Syd suggested that we might like to pay a flying visit to another island which he and others were going to develop as a leisure complex for big game fishermen and wealthy tourists. It was a little jewel of an island set in the sparkling waters of the Coral Sea, uninhabited except for a couple of workmen and quite a number of large monitor-type lizards.

We were taken out fishing on the cabin cruiser which was moored off a beautiful sandy beach and almost as soon as we dropped our hand lines over the side the bait was taken by coral trout. There were several hooks on each of our lines and they were all occupied – if that is the right word – by these large fish. A barbecue had been set up on shore and it was soon grilling our catches, gutted and wrapped in tin-foil. They tasted absolutely delicious and we washed them down with a very smooth Australian claret. Andrew and Jennifer went snorkelling, safe in the knowledge that the outer reef protected them from sharks. Myra, David and Katy went looking for shells and I just lay in the sand like a beached whale soaking up the sun, claret oozing from every pore. A day like that will linger long in the memory and even longer in the liver.

The next time I visited Lizard Island was to perform at the newly finished, very exclusive leisure complex into which it had been transformed. I had promised Syd Williams – now Sir Sydney – that I would bring a show along, complete with orchestra, to mark the opening. We decided between us that it would be a black-tie affair and that it should be televised. After that it began to take on the appearance of a national event. A Royal Australian Navy frigate turned up and its ratings formed a guard of honour for the Premier of Queensland Jo Bjelke Peterson who flew in to the brand new airstrip for the occasion. Guests came in from all over the place, some by air and some by boat, and champagne flowed like water. A somewhat bizarre occasion considering we were in the middle of nowhere, but everyone had a good time and the rising sun found several dinner-jacketed guests asleep on the sand.

A lot of good things happened to me in Australia, including my silver wedding anniversary and the announcement of my knighthood, and I have accumulated many, many friends. I made a farewell tour three years ago, but I have promised to return with Myra on our golden wedding anniversary in 1998 just to visit my old Aussie mates and Beryl Kennedy, Bob's widow, who is now living there with her son.

Many of my tours Down Under have included side trips to New Zealand where there are some fine concert halls. Christchurch Town Hall in particular has magnificent acoustics. In comparison, the first time I played the old

Wellington Town Hall about twenty-five years ago, there were cries of 'We can't hear you, mate', from certain parts of the auditorium. Normally I don't get that kind of reaction because my voice has the piercing quality of a laser beam when I'm in full throttle. Apparently there were dead spots in the hall where the cheaper seats were. There was nothing I could do about it apart from going around to those who couldn't hear me and singing to them individually which would have probably deafened them. However, the last time I played Wellington I performed in a new concert hall with a great sound system and an audience to match.

New Zealand folk are more reserved than the Aussies and a little more formal. I remember playing an open air theatre in South Island which had an ornamental pond between the front of the stage and the first rows of seats. The audience had come prepared with blankets and thermos flasks which surprised me when I saw them settling themselves down before the show began. The day had been reasonably warm and I wondered why the public were muffled up. It was still daylight when the show started, then as the sun went down a mist began to rise above the little lake in front of the stage. By the time it was my turn to go on, moths and other flying creatures fluttered about in the spotlight just as they had done in Parkes when we did a night shoot, and it was difficult to make out the audience through the miasma before me. Fortunately the sound system was in good order thanks to Billy Rowe my road manager, and though my facial expressions were lost in the fuzzy, moth-ridden stage lighting, my voice was coming through loud and strong. I sang my heart out that night and in spite of the fact that most of my gags were greeted with polite applause, the songs went down very well and people stamped their feet at the end of each ballad. I commented on this to Billy Rowe after the show. 'Don't fool yourself, Harry,' he said. 'They were trying to keep their feet warm.' Mind you, he was grinning when he said it.

During my tours in New Zealand we covered a lot of territory, visiting places like Dunedin, Invercargill, Nelson, New Plymouth, Auckland and everywhere we went we were made very welcome, especially by the ex-pats to whom we brought a touch of home. It's a long way to go and I have to confess that when Myra and the kids were not with me I often felt very alone. I would sometimes stand on some lonely beach surrounded by every kind of tropical beauty and look yearningly across the sea, wishing that I were back in noisy old Cheam Road with the bus stop opposite and the bus conductor calling out 'Harry's corner!'

Entertaining the Services

There is a saying amongst old Royal Artillerymen which goes, 'once a gunner, always a gunner', and there's a lot of truth in that. I don't mean that every ex-gunner should keep a twenty-five pound artillery piece in his garden – there's enough trouble about hand guns in private ownership as it is. What the saying refers to is that the comradeship forged in battle lasts one's whole life.

That is why I have always had a soft spot for the Army, and so whenever I have been asked to entertain the Services I have gone willingly, with the result that I have been to nearly every trouble spot that our soldiers have been involved in.

Together with Eric Sykes I visited Kenya in 1952 when the Mau Mau uprising was on. The hairiest part of that trip was after our outbound plane had landed at Rome for refuelling and took off again for Nairobi. The starboard engine of our South African Airways DC7 feathered itself and blew up. This meant that we had to go back to Rome, but before we could do so, the fuel we had taken on board had to be jettisoned.

As we circled above the Eternal City with all the plane's

lights switched off because of the danger of St Elmo's fire, Eric and I opened a bottle of Italian brandy I had bought at the airport and, as the aircraft ditched its load of aviation spirit, we were taking on board quite a large amount of another liquid. Eric had his guitar with him and we regaled our fellow passengers with what I suppose could be called a 'spirited' rendition of 'The Banana Boat Song', about the only tune Eric was able to play.

By the time we had landed back at Rome there were fire engines and ambulances waiting for us, but my friend and I tripped down the landing steps without a care in the world – until the next day when we both had terrible hangovers. We were stranded in Rome for two days while we waited for a spare engine to be sent up from South Africa, but the rest of our journey was nothing like as eventful, thank God.

I took another trip to Kenya a year or two later with Norman Vaughan and Harry Worth – two of my best mates. The only thing that bugged me about my companions at the time was their apparent indifference to what was going on around them. They spent a lot of their spare time reminiscing about old Variety performers with whom they had worked, while I was wide-eyed with wonder and fascination at the sights and sounds around us. In Cyprus, the first stop on our tour, I was always looking for subjects for my ever-present camera. Harry and Norman would give me a cheery wave, declining my offer of a trip out to some exciting archaeological dig, preferring the comfort of the sergeants' mess.

When we got to Kenya, we did a show at the Bell Inn on the shore of Lake Naivasha, where we were staying. It was the most beautiful spot, and the flamingos on the lake shone pinkly in the setting sun as I wandered down to the lakeside in the early evening before the show was due to start. To my surprise, Harry and Norman had beaten me to it and were sitting on a bench facing this spectacular scene.

'They've got the message at last,' I thought happily as I crept up behind them.

'Now, Sandy Powell,' Harry was saying. 'There was a funny man . . .' I left them to it.

I have done many shows in Nissen huts, on rickety, temporary stages – even from the backs of Army trucks – from Northern Ireland to the Far East, with some excellent travelling companions – people like Anita Harris, who came with me on several CSE trips and was always great company; and an excellent comic called Kenny Cantor, who has worked with me both here and in Australia and, incidentally, was responsible for me becoming a member of the Grand Order of Water Rats, a show business charity – but there are two outstanding occasions which I want particularly to mention. The first one was the time I went down to visit the Services in the Falklands.

When the war in the Falklands was over, I was asked to head a British Forces Broadcasting Services concert party to entertain the lads down there. I agreed immediately – after all, we had won the war and I was keen to see what the place looked like. The party consisted of Jack Honeyborne, my accompanist, Bryan Marshall, a very good young comic, Joan Hinde, who can play the trumpet like the Archangel Gabriel himself, and two pretty, young singers. Tony Boyd, Jimmy Grafton's assistant, also came with us to help with the staging of the show. Derek Agutter, Jenny's father and an old friend from previous tours, was in charge of the operation.

The first part of the journey was fine. We boarded a VC-10 at RAF Brize Norton and left for Ascension Island, arriving there in the middle of the night. I sat up front for the landing, marvelling at how the pilot and navigator could find this tiny speck in the Atlantic, and feeling extremely relieved when they did.

After we went through the usual formalities, I was driven by the station Commander up to his house on the hill, where

I was to be his guest for the night. It was pitch black dark and I couldn't see a thing on the way, but my host insisted on pointing out various beauty spots which I could look out for in the morning. When we got to his place we sat and chatted for quite a while over a cup of tea. He explained that the flight down to Port Stanley would be by a Hercules air transport plane, which would have to be refuelled in mid-air because it could not carry enough fuel to make the journey.

The tanker plane was a Vulcan bomber which had been adapted for the purpose. If we missed the rendezvous somewhere over the South Atlantic, or the weather was bad over Port Stanley, we would have to go back to Ascension Island and start again. He also told me that the last flight that had gone, a couple of days previously, had made two attempts before it eventually landed in Port Stanley. I thanked him for the information and went to bed where I lay rigid and sleepless until daybreak.

We made our rendezvous with no problems, thank God, and I joined the crew on the flight deck for the refuelling. The pilot explained that the top speed of the Hercules was stalling speed for the Vulcan, so the operation had to be performed in a dive.

The Vulcan circled us and released a fuel line from under its fuselage. At the end of the hose was a device into which the probe on the nose of our aircraft had to fit to take the fuel on board. It was a complicated operation, relying on the fine expertise of both pilots, but it was completed with no bother at all, and everybody on board cheered when it was over.

The Hercules, by the way, is essentially a transport plane, and passenger comfort is a low priority. We sat where we could, on whatever piece of equipment looked most comfortable, but no one complained, although we were all glad to disembark at Port Stanley airport, where our welcome was warm and everybody was looking forward to the shows.

Memories of the battle were still fresh and we were told some hair raising stories of the ill-treatment of the young and inexperienced Argentine soldiers by their officers. Towards the end of the conflict, some of these youngsters were starving while their officers had a stockpile of rations which they kept to themselves.

Rex Hunt, who was the Governor at the time of the invasion, showed me around Government House, pointing out the bullet holes in the walls from the first attack. Then he produced something quite remarkable. The official Government visitor's book had been signed by all the high-ranking Argentine officers. Rex left for England before we did our first show. Perhaps he'd had enough trouble.

We did shows in all sorts of places – in hangars, sheds – in fact wherever Jack Honeyborne could plug in his electric piano. We performed on Merchant ships and Royal Navy vessels, and our audiences were more than kind. The final show was at Port Stanley Town Hall, the first time that the local population had seen any kind of entertainment since the occupation.

The mines that the Argentines had laid so indiscriminately made travelling anywhere on the main island very hazardous and new mine maps were issued at regular intervals, and for this reason we had to travel by helicopter quite often.

I have to say that I was very proud of the way the members of the show put up with the rigours of battling against a constant wind and having such primitive conditions in which to work. Joan Hinde was particularly stoical and never complained. Neither did Jack Honeyborne. A very droll man at the best of times, he didn't make too much fuss when he fell off an improvised stage one night when I was singing a top note. When he came back up again he was wearing ear protectors.

At the time we were there, in May 1983, quite a few soldiers were billeted with the locals, and we heard tales of some of the lads lighting fires first thing in the morning and generally being helpful in the home. After a while though, to avoid the inevitable friction between the younger members of the community and the more sophisticated servicemen, a huge complex was built around the airport at Mount Pleasant which could accommodate the servicemen and provide them with television and more of the comforts of home, leaving the local inhabitants to get on with their lives. When I returned in 1986 with *Highway*, the new complex had already been completed, apparently, in record time.

I was struck by the very British lifestyles of the Falklanders. I remember being entertained to tea at a farmhouse in Goose Green. It was just like being back in 1930s England, with an Aga stove in the kitchen and a little boy in flannel pyjamas and a woollen dressing-gown, with little carpet slippers on his feet, sitting on the fender in front of the fire, watching his mother, in a flowered pinafore, busying herself making the tea and arranging home-made scones on decorated plates. It brought back memories of the times when I was home from school with a cold and watching my mother getting the table ready for tea.

Other things which had not changed were the stink of cordite and the sight of empty shell cases and old field-dressing bandages littering green, windswept fields. As the song goes, 'When will they ever learn?'

The second outstanding tour I was involved in came about after I received a letter from the man in charge of Forces Entertainment. The letter said that I was invited to go out to the Gulf to meet some of the servicemen and try to spread some Christmas cheer, even though the Christmas season was a few weeks off. Apparently the lads were sitting around down there in Saudi Arabia waiting to have a go at Saddam Hussein and needed to see a familiar face from home. I thought at first that the army had the idea that if I sang a few choruses of 'We'll Keep a Welcome' within earshot of

Saddam's front line troops, they might think twice about hanging around in Kuwait. But when Julie Stephens, my secretary at the time, made a few discreet enquiries, she was told that I was not expected to sing because not even the combined efforts of myself and Des O'Connor would shift Saddam in his present unpredictable mood.

And so it was that I presented myself at RAF Brize Norton with just an overnight bag for the flight down to Riyadh. I also met up with the gentleman from British Forces Broadcasting who was to accompany me.

When I presented my passport at the flight desk, there was some consternation at the fact that it included an Israeli visa, due to the fact that I had been out there to record three *Highway* programmes. Saudi Arabia does not admit anyone with an Israeli visa. Messages whizzed to and fro between Brize Norton and Riyadh and eventually I was given some kind of diplomatic immunity.

The next thing was the briefing, which took place in the lounge at the RAF airport. I'm pretty used to this sort of thing, having made many trips abroad for the services, but this briefing had a chilling message. The officer instructing us told us that due to the possibility that Saddam might decide to launch a nerve gas attack, we all had to try on the protective suits and masks with which we were provided and which had to be carried around with us at all times. The equipment was duly produced, and I had some difficulty struggling into mine. The gas mask was the most important item. Apparently one had only about ten seconds to get it on before one became contaminated. This put something of a damper on the previously light-hearted atmosphere in the lounge, and I began to wonder if I'd been a bit hasty in agreeing to make the trip. I even had the idea of ringing Bob Kennedy to tell him to check the small print in my insurance policy. I knew that there was something in it about an 'Act of God', and I hoped that Saddam did not come under that category, even if *he* thought he did.

We were given plenty of time to practise getting in and out of the decontamination suits and, having realized how essential they were to life preservation, I would have made Robert Nesbitt proud at the speed with which I made the quick change.

Eventually we were escorted to the aircraft and made welcome by the RAF flight attendants who were jolly but firm about the procedures that were to be undertaken in the event of something unexpected happening during the flight. The other passengers, being mostly air crew – pilots, navigators, etc. – took it all in their stride, while I sat, a 71-year-old ex-gunner, veteran of a war light-years removed from this new one which might happen at any time, pondering on the reception I might receive from the young soldiers who were out in the desert preparing to face Saddam with every conceivable kind of modern weapons system which made our old 25-pounder guns seem as antiquated as bows and arrows.

On the plane, a young navigator approached me and asked if I remembered him from Barbados. As a matter of fact I did, just. The last time I had seen him he was a little lad who used to play football with my kids on the beach at Settlers Beach on the St James's Coast. He was then known as Tiger, and he was David Coleman's son.

I wished him well and he grinned and gave me the thumbs up as he went back to his seat. I suddenly felt very old and sad, and tears welled up in my eyes.

The flight was a long one because we were flying in a military aircraft and had to keep to a flight plan which kept us from flying over certain countries. When we landed I was amazed at the amount of military aircraft around us, but I was given no time to linger, and was whisked off the plane and into a car which took me and my companion from BFBS straight to the Embassy, where we were to spend what was left of the night.

I was given a very comfortable room in which cold drinks and fruit awaited me, along with a welcoming note from the Ambassador inviting me to have breakfast with him before I left for the next leg of the journey up to the area where I was to start meeting the lads.

I seemed only to have slept for a few moments before I was woken with a cup of tea and the news that breakfast would be ready in half an hour. I changed into the light clothes I had brought over and trotted downstairs to meet the Ambassador. He was a charming man and we got on like a house on fire. He even loaned me a floppy hat to protect my bald spot from the sun which, he warned me, was going to be very fierce.

The next flight was by Hercules aircraft to Al Jubayl, where there was more evidence of the tremendous build-up of planes and equipment, and a greater sense of urgency, which always deepens the nearer you get to where the action might be. I remembered this very well from the battles I had been involved in and I began to get the same old churning in the stomach, together with a sort of suppressed excitement.

Time now to meet the servicemen at my first port of call and try to raise a smile or two. There was a bit of embarrassed shuffling for a few moments as I was introduced to them, but to my relief we all had a laugh together as they got used to me. I posed for photographs and signed various pieces of paper – 'it's not for me, it's for my mum' – and then a cheery wave, and off to the next place.

It all became a kaleidoscope picture of shaking hands, asking where the lads came from – 'anyone here from Wales?'

'I've got an auntie who lived next door to you in Maesteg.' I never lived there, but smile and nod anyway.

'My mum always watches you on *Songs of Praise*.' I resist

the temptation to say 'No, I'm on *Highway*,' glad at least that they know me from somewhere, they're too young for the Goons.

Then a welcome cry of 'Ying tong iddle I po' from the older blokes, and 'Give my regards to Spike' – they all know him.

'What are you doing out here, mate?' No answer to that one.

'Saw you when you came out to Cyprus or Belfast, or Port Stanley . . .' Shoulders back a bit at that.

'Like a brew-up, bombardier?' Ah, that's more like it.

Brigadier Cordingley, the man in command of 7th Armoured Brigade, escorted me personally around the heavy gun artillery positions further up in the desert towards where the front line would be when the fireworks began. He was the antithesis of the common concept of a brigadier. For a start, he volunteered to carry my heavy camera and asked me seriously what it was like to be in action. Having often been under fire during my service in the war, I could speak from experience, although only in the capacity of a walk-on part. I answered, 'How's your sphincter muscle?'

There was a lot of compassion in the man and he was obviously a favourite with those who served under him. We chatted about opera, about which he was far more knowledgeable than I, and when we parted, after a ride in one of his tanks, I thought to myself that I would have been very happy to have been under his command. Not *now*, of course, but when I was a soldier.

Later, when the balloon went up, he acquitted himself very well indeed, and is now Major-General Patrick Cordingley, DSO, and deservedly so.

The idea was for me to visit all three services, and after being with the 7th Armoured Brigade, I was taken by helicopter out to HMS *Cardiff*, which was on duty off Kuwait. By this time I had a couple of minders and the BFBS man with me, and away we went to land on the ship while it was cruising along – a most interesting experience, to say the least.

I was shown around the ship – which was then on some kind of constant alert – and I managed to meet most of the ship's company. Below decks there was a bewildering array of computer equipment, which I was only allowed a brief look at, and then we all had tea in the Captain's cabin. Like most of the officers in all three services with whom I came into contact, he seemed remarkably young for such a high command, but there was no doubt about his ability.

We piled back into the helicopter for the return journey feeling pretty good about things and looking forward to lunch ashore. Then, out of the blue, all hell broke loose in the cockpit and the easygoing crew suddenly became terrifyingly efficient and our helicopter descended towards sea level as the pilot issued terse commands into his headset.

We jigged about over the sea for a while, until he seemed to get some reassurance that all was well and we returned to our previous height. I was just about getting my heart back to where it was supposed to be, when the same thing happened all over again. The pilot followed the same procedure and down we went to sea level. The first time it happened I had a faint suspicion that it might have been a bit of a 'send-up', to give me something to talk about when I got home, but there was no denying the seriousness of the pilot's behaviour the second time.

After we had returned to our proper height again, the pilot told us that a missile had locked on to us twice and he had had to drop down to sea level in order to confuse the missile's homing in mechanism.

'So that's what it was,' I remarked calmly as I disentangled myself from the navigator's lap, wondering where I could change my underwear.

Months later, I found out what the fuss was about when I

was invited to lunch at Chequers by the Prime Minister. I was on the same table as General Sir Peter de la Billière, and he explained that a Saudi naval frigate had not been alerted that a helicopter was leaving HMS *Cardiff* and had prepared a missile launch when said helicopter appeared on its radar screen. So, thanks to the quick thinking of the pilot, an international incident was avoided.

If you think I'm kidding, this is all noted by the general in his book.

After I had finished what the Army had referred to as a 'grip and grin' visit, I went back to Riyadh for a barbecue with a lot of service personnel at the staff military attaché's house. As it was getting near to Christmas, we all sang carols in his garden. I was delighted to see the Ambassador again and return his hat. To my surprise, he had a fine baritone voice and together we belted out the old favourite carols until we were hoarse.

It was a night to remember in many ways. There we were, celebrating a Christian festival in the heart of an Arab country under a sky studded with stars – just as it might have looked from that stable in Bethlehem. There we were, singing songs about peace on earth and goodwill to mankind, and yet, not far away, young men were readying themselves for a war which could come at any time.

Later that night, as we flew back to Brize Norton, my head was crowded with the events of the past twenty-four hours, and I remember saying a silent prayer for the safety of all the people I had met. Sadly, the young Lancashire Fusilier who had driven us around Riyadh was killed by 'friendly fire' when the battle for Kuwait began, some weeks after my visit.

I worry sometimes that these overseas trips for the services are regarded as self-publicity exercises which do little to lift the morale for the rank and file, and I begin to question my motives. And then I get a letter from a lad's parents, saying how much their son enjoyed meeting me – and I feel better about it.

I was to get more involved with the Army when, one evening in my dressing-room at the Palladium, I happened to remark to one of my regular visitors, Arthur Watson, that I seemed to be getting quite a lot of requests to perform at midnight matinées for the RAF Benevolent Fund. Arthur, along with George Brightwell, had run Combined Services Entertainment.

'Is there an Army Benevolent Fund?' I asked him. 'If so, I'm sure that a lot of performers who had served in khaki would be delighted to help it earn a few bob.'

In no time I was knee-deep in generals, all of them connected with the ABF and ready to listen to any ideas I might have. They were really splendid chaps and not in any way like some senior officers I had met in my period in the services.

In due course, the idea was born of a Sunday concert in a West End theatre with contributions from as many ex-Army performers as we could get, with all the proceeds going to the ABF. The show was to be called 'Fall in the Stars' and the venue was the Victoria Palace. Billy Chappell, an ex-captain and a brilliant choreographer and director of ballets and West End revues, was to be the producer. I had met Billy when he came backstage to see me after an Army show in Rome in which I was the lead comedian. He said then that the next time he'd see me would be in the West End. When he turned up to see me at the Palladium ten years later I said 'Where have you been till now?'

The show was a great success and was the forerunner of many more. One particular senior officer, Brigadier Gerry Landy, became a great personal friend. He really should have been in the theatre – he has a genius for organization and always gets what he wants without ever raising his voice.

Mind you, so does Myra.

It was always a secret thrill for me to be able to call these generals by their first names, and the first time I was invited to an Army Council dinner I felt quite chuffed as I dressed for the occasion, proud of my cluster of medals and the emblem of a Commander of the British Empire around my neck.

When I arrived, the first person I met was Field Marshal Lord Templar, who had so many medals and decorations that there was hardly enough room for them all. I was glad to retire to a corner of the room with my pathetic collection. My humiliation was complete when my brand new CBE became unstuck and dropped into the soup, which happened to be Brown Windsor — somehow making the incident doubly *lèse-majesté*.

On the Highway

One day in 1983, I received a letter which led to a big change in my career. It was from Bill Ward, who I had worked with in television for many years, and who had been responsible for wooing me away from the BBC to the newly established Associated Television Company when Independent Television first started. In the letter, he asked if he could take me to lunch to talk about an idea he had for a television series.

We met for lunch in the restaurant of the Stafford Hotel, which is conveniently situated around the corner from my office in St James's Place. There were only the two of us and, after we had spent some time chatting about mutual acquaintances and shared reminiscences, Bill came out with the reason for our meeting. He told me that there was a plan to put out a series of programmes of a religious nature, to be broadcast on a Sunday evening in what was known as the 'God Slot'. The content of these programmes was to include plenty of music and interviews with interesting people, and they were to come from a different region of the country every week. 'And we want you to present the programme,' said Bill, leaning back in his chair and looking me straight in the eye.

I was, to say the least of it, flabbergasted. I had sung lots of hymns and sacred songs on *Stars on Sunday*, and I had once presented a children's programme about Easter called *The Cross on the Donkey's Back*, but I was not a heavily religious person myself. I also thought that my long association with the *Goon Shows* was not quite the right background for a presenter of the kind of programme he had in mind. Bill didn't agree.

'You don't have to be a "guru",' he said. 'We'd just like you to sing a couple of hymns and interview interesting people who have done good things for those around them. Turning the spotlight on the unsung saints in the community, if you like. It will be more about caring than about religion and we see it as inter-faith and inter-denominational.'

I was intrigued by the suggestion and said that I would think about it. The one thing that worried me was that I did not want to be seen as a 'holier than thou' kind of presenter. What I thought was that I would act as a 'Mr Everyman', asking questions which the average viewer would like answered. I certainly would not be blowing raspberries, but at the same time I would still be myself as the viewing public knew me.

It was eventually agreed that I would give it a try, and Jimmy Grafton arranged a contract for six programmes, with a view to extending them if all went well. I was delighted to find that my old mate, Ronnie Cass, a fellow Welshman from Llanelli, was going to be the musical associate on *Highway*. I had worked with Ronnie on many television shows, mostly the *Secombe With Music* programmes with Peter Knight and his orchestra from Yorkshire Television. He knows my voice better than I do and coaxes performances from me that I never thought I could possibly achieve.

The first two programmes came from the Tyne Tees Television area, primarily because that was the station from which the show was to be administered. The first show was a Remembrance Sunday *Highway* from Durham Cathedral and the chief guest was Wendy Craig, who was to appear several times during the life of the programme.

In the beginning I found it strange to be the interviewer and not the interviewee, though chatting to Wendy, an old friend, made things easier. Another strange thing was having to speak into the camera lens and address the viewing audience directly. The only way I could do this without freezing up was to imagine that I was just talking to one particular family, and I gradually got used to the idea. Obviously, I was no stranger to the camera lens, but I had previously been Harry Secombe the comic and though I wanted to retain some of that identity, I would also have to be taken seriously when the occasion demanded. In addition, I had to learn all the links within the programme by heart, something I did not always manage to do, as my frequent appearances on Denis Norden's *It'll Be All Right On the Night* will testify.

One thing I did learn early on was to put at ease the person I was going to interview, and the best way to do this was to have a cup of tea and a chat beforehand. This was most important as the majority of people were terrified of the prospect of going before the television cameras. They all had a good story to tell and it was in their interest and the interest of the programme that they were presented in the best possible light. This was much easier when, after we had done a few series, a mobile caravan was provided for me, in which I had a place where I could be made up and where I could meet the folk I was going to interview. It was good to be able to go over what they were going to say and gradually calm them down. I would have all the information about the interviewees from the researchers in the region in which we were working, and I'd know from the director what area he would like the interview to cover. Naturally, as time went by

I became used to the technique, but in those first programmes I was usually more nervous than those I was attempting to settle down.

The first six programmes went very well indeed and more were commissioned, until *Highway* became firmly established and began to give *Songs of Praise*, which went out at the same time on Sunday evening on BBC 1, some healthy competition.

Highway was a unique programme because it came from eleven different regions – Tyne Tees, Border, Grampian, Scottish Television, HTV Wales, HTV Bristol, Anglia, Channel, Ulster, TV South and TSW. Each region provided its own director, researchers, wardrobe and make-up, camera crew, lighting and sound people. The Central Unit, which was based in London at the Tyne Tees Television offices, consisted of Bill Ward as executive producer, Ronnie Cass as musical associate and script writer, a secretary and myself. To ensure that no two programmes contained the same ingredients, the scripts were sent to us in advance, often accompanied by the director. Ronnie would then consult with each regional musical director about what hymns or sacred songs were to be recorded.

Once *Highway* had been going for a couple of years, the music was always recorded at CTS Studios in Wembley. We had the finest session musicians in the country to play for us under the baton of Ted Brennan who, with Ronnie, did all the arrangements, apart from those done by the incomparable Peter Knight in the early days of the programme.

Perhaps I should explain why the music had to be pre-recorded. First of all, it would be rather difficult to conceal an eighteen-piece orchestra behind a couple of trees when I sang a ballad in a sylvan setting, or to have a male voice choir following me down the street as I belted out 'Onward Christian Soldiers', and so, in order to achieve a balanced sound, the music had to be recorded under studio conditions. Secondly, for the same reasons, I had to sing in the studio, too. This meant that I had to mime to the pre-recorded sound relayed by speakers strategically placed out of sight of the cameras. Now, it looks a bit phoney when the singer just opens and closes his mouth in synchronization with the words, without making a sound. Under normal circumstances, for example, I go a funny colour when I hit a top C, so if I appear to sing a high note with no apparent effort, the viewers will automatically say 'Hey up! He's not singing – he's miming', and they think they're being cheated. It has always been done that way in film musicals and has been accepted by the general public, but on television, for some reason, one cannot always get away with it. That's why I take great care that my lip movements coincide as near as possible with those I made in the studio, and I can do this by actually singing along with the recorded sound, so at least I can be seen making an effort.

I remember one snowy day somewhere in Dorset when I had to sing 'Trees' alongside a fast-flowing stream, the sound of which almost drowned out the music being played through the concealed speakers. When I had finished – after about half a dozen goes at it – I climbed wearily up the bank, encrusted with snow, to be confronted by a large lady, with an almost equally large dog, who had been watching the filming. 'Why are you not singing properly?' she said, pointing an accusing finger at me. 'You're doing it the easy way.'

I straightened up indignantly, preparing to discuss the pros and cons of singing unaccompanied in a snowstorm, when I lost my balance and slipped backwards down the bank.

'Serves you right!' she cried and marched off.

I think she must have seen *Song of Norway*.

Highway soon became a new way of life for me. I met so many fine people – ordinary folk who had done extraordinary things – that I began to realize that, contrary to what the tabloid headlines seem to indicate, there is a tremendous amount of good being done, quietly and without thought of reward, throughout the country. Previously, when I had toured the provincial theatres, I rarely came into contact with the people who lived in the towns because the nature of our profession confines one to the journey from the digs to the theatre and back again, with the occasional round of golf thrown in. One never gets to meet the audience individually, except for the autograph hunters at the stage door, and one leaves a town without getting to know anything about it or those who live in it.

It was different with *Highway*. I got to learn a lot about towns and cities at grassroots level, and listened to stories of triumph in the face of dreadful adversity. Like the experiences of Cantor Ernest Levy of Glasgow, who had been in eleven different concentration camps in Germany during the war and yet felt no bitterness for those who had treated him so harshly. As he told his story, simply and with no histrionics, all those of us involved in the recording were in tears. There was a shining sincerity in the man that transcended all the evil that had been done to him, adding a new dimension to what tolerance and forgiveness really mean.

I had the privilege of interviewing and presenting many inspirational characters during the ten years of *Highway*, but here are a few extra special ones that I will always remember.

I first met Evelyn Glennie in a programme we recorded for Grampian Television in Royal Deeside. She was introduced to me as a musician who was profoundly deaf, but who had an amazing facility to lip read. Her lip reading was so good that if she was addressed as 'Eevelyn', with a long 'ee', and not 'Evelyn', with a short 'e', she would politely correct one's pronunciation. She has the most attractive and vibrant personality and, after a chat with me in the church at Balmoral, she played the piano for us. She said in the interview that her ambition was to teach music to deaf children. She also mentioned that she was a percussionist, and in later programmes we found out what a superb percussion and xylophone player she was. She went on to become a regular member of the *Highway* orchestra and from there became an internationally renowned musician and won the 'Scots Woman of the Decade' award. She is now in constant demand around the world, but she is still the modest girl we met in Deeside.

Another remarkable lady who appeared on a *Highway* from Edinburgh was Carolyn James who, after being partially sighted for many years, became completely blind. The amazing thing about Carolyn is that she is a very accomplished watercolourist with many exhibitions to her credit. In addition, she has developed a talent for lyric writing and, in association with Ronnie Cass, who has written the music to her lyrics, she has had many of her songs performed by Dana, Ian Wallace and myself.

In a *Highway* from Gloucester we introduced a Mrs Denise Cole who had a miraculous story to tell. She had been suffering from MS for some years and was confined to a wheelchair. One day she went to a local church service and became a born again Christian. Some time later, she joined a group of fellow worshippers who were going on a trip to the Holy Land, sponsored by her church. She was determined that when they got to Jerusalem she would walk, with a walking frame, the length of the Via Dolorosa, the route taken by Jesus on his way to be crucified. For her it was going to be an act of faith, purely and simply.

But something truly miraculous happened to her that day. She told me that she suffered excruciating pain as she struggled along the narrow road and, by the time she reached her goal, she was about to pass out. Then, quite suddenly, the pain left her completely and she found that she could walk unaided. The shock of this happening to her made her afraid to tell anyone about it in case it was a temporary remission. However, she began to realize that she really had recovered the use of her legs and she told the others around her of her miracle.

She has completely recovered from her MS and has since dedicated her life to helping others with the same condition. There seems to be no medical explanation for her sudden recovery. Temporary remissions do occur in some cases of multiple sclerosis, but Denise's recovery has long outgrown the period of other remissions.

In the programme we were both sitting down during the interview, only to realize after the show had been transmitted that we had not taken the opportunity to show Denise's ability to walk about. So it was decided that when we recorded our special Christmas show I would introduce her and the two of us would waltz around the studio together, just to prove that we had not been telling 'fibs'. Ronnie Cass had written a 'Mrs Cole's Waltz' especially for the occasion.

Then there was the lovely Laura Morris of Caerphilly, who beat off lymph cancer, became an air hostess and now devotes all her spare time to raising money for the hospital that helped to cure her.

Two doctors, from different parts of the country but both blessed with the same gift of compassion, made a big impression on me in two separate programmes.

The first was Dr Peter Griffiths, who was featured in a *Highway* from HTV Wales. He had given up a lucrative practice in south London to found and maintain a hospice in Tŷ Olwen near Swansea. I always felt like an intruder when we filmed patients in hospitals, especially when they were terminally ill, so I was prepared for a hushed atmosphere and long faces when we went along to Tŷ Olwen. The scene that met us could not have been more different. There was laughter in the wards and dogs wandered in and out between the beds, as Dr Griffiths believed that his patients could have anything that they wanted, within reason, to ease their last days, and had no objection to well-loved pets being brought into the hospital so that their owners could wish them farewell.

Dr Griffiths spoke of his 'little triumphs', such as allowing a patient to go home to attend a wedding even though he knew that he only had a couple of days left. Like a lot of doctors who tend to the terminally ill, he believed in counselling the family about how to cope with the coming bereavement and, although he had to administer pain-killing medicine, he was determined that his patients would die with dignity and not in a drug-induced coma.

The other doctor, Dr Lloyd, runs a premature baby unit in an Aberdeen hospital. His charges are so tiny that at first sight it is hard to believe that they are human, they look just like little dolls as they lie in their incubators. When I said this to Dr Lloyd, he smiled and said, 'That's why we dress them in dolls' outfits, to give the little souls some kind of dignity when the parents come in to see them.'

He takes a keen interest in the babies after they leave his care and is proud of every one of them. When you see photographs of some of these wee scraps of humanity just after their birth and then compare them with the sturdy boys and girls of a couple of years later, you realize that he and his staff have every reason to be proud.

Jenny Rees-Larcombe was a lady we met in a programme from Tunbridge Wells. She was a patient at Burswood, a centre which combines spiritual healing with orthodox medicine and comes under the aegis of the Archbishop of Canterbury. At that time she was suffering from encephalitis and was confined to a wheelchair. When I interviewed her, she had refused to take any pain-killing drugs that day so that she could speak coherently. She told me that she had come to Burswood hoping for a miracle but had, instead, settled for the lesser miracle of coming to terms with what had happened to her. She spoke of how angry and frustrated she had been when she was first stricken by her illness, how her attitude had changed during her stay at the centre, and how she had found an inner peace. It was a most moving interview and one that remained with me long after the programme went out.

Then, several months later, the *Highway* office received a letter from Jenny telling us that she had been completely cured of her encephalitis.

Apparently, she had gone to a Christian meeting where prayers were being offered for the sick and a young girl asked Jenny whether she minded if she prayed for her. Jenny said she had no objection, and this young girl then said a prayer for Jenny to be cured. To her great surprise, Jenny felt her illness leave her to such an extent that she found that she could walk home unaided. Her recovery was complete and has remained so.

There is one other lady I have to mention. No miracles happened to her, but, instead, by sheer strength of character and faith in God, she overcame tremendous physical handicap. She is Hilary MacDowell from an Ulster Television *Highway*. Hilary was born severely disabled and seemed doomed to spend her life in a wheelchair. Her parents were told that she would never be able to walk and that she could never go to school. Hilary was so determined to beat these odds against her, that she got the other members of her family to teach her what they learned at school and then set about teaching herself to walk. She succeeded so brilliantly that she now has a PhD from the Open University, is a deacon of her local church and runs a street theatre group in Donaghadee.

There are so many other *Highway* stories of people who have demonstrated the power of faith over seemingly insurmountable adversity, that it would be impossible to list them all. Remember, we did over 365 programmes in the ten years that *Highway* was on the air.

We shed a lot of tears during the making of some of those shows, but we also had plenty of laughs along the way. I have never believed that religion should be a grimly serious affair, after all, it is natural to assume that as Christ and his disciples spent so much time together, as well as praying together, they must have laughed together.

There is a traditional prayer that is always heard at the annual Clowns' Service and it was recited on a *Highway* from Monmouth by little Luke Mumford.

Dear Lord, I thank you for calling me to share with others your precious gift of laughter.

May I never forget that it is your gift and my privilege.

As your children are rebuked in their self-importance and cheered in their sadness, let me remember that your foolishness is wiser than men's wisdom.

We covered around 25,000 miles a year during the time *Highway* was going, and there were plenty of things which should not have gone wrong but which, of course, did.

We went to Rome with Border Television for two *Highway*s, one of which was to be a special Easter programme in which I was to try to get an Easter message from the Pope.

I found it great fun to be filming in some of the famous Roman places of interest, like the Fountain of Trevi and the Castel di Sant Angelo, where I sang 'E lucevan le stelle' – 'The Stars Are Brightly Shining' – from Puccini's *Tosca* from the very cell in which the scene was set in the opera.

It was 'nostalgia time' for me because I had spent some time in Rome after I had finished playing walk-on parts in the Italian campaign in 1944. Now I was able to see the city in a different light. I remembered entering St Peter's Cathedral, looking in awe at the magnificence around me, as my army boots rang out on the marble floor. This time I was there to sing, with the Vatican choir backing me, the lovely 'Agnus Dei'. We had pre-recorded the music, as we always did, and I was glad we had done so, because inside the Cathedral there was an echo that seemed to go on and on, making it quite difficult to mime. However, Aled Jones seemed to have no trouble with it when he sang his solo, once again proving what a great musician he is.

The interview with His Holiness had been set up in the auditorium of the Vatican and I had been allotted a seat in the front row. The camera had been sited so that as the Pope walked along he would be in sharp focus when he got to me. A microphone, powerful enough to pick up both our voices, had been fixed to the front of my jacket. In the background, by the camera, Bill Ward stood with Bill Cartner, the Border Television director, ready to give me the signal that the camera was running.

The auditorium was packed with people from all over the world and the atmosphere was more like that of a Wembley Cup Final, with banners waving and lots of chanting going on.

Those in the front pews, who were given the honour of actually shaking hands with His Holiness, had senior members of the Catholic Church sitting beside them to effect the introduction. Unfortunately, the Monsignor who was to look after me had not turned up. We found out later that the poor man had flu. As the Pope got nearer to me, Bill Ward began waving his arms about to give me the signal that the camera was now recording the action. By this time, I was going over in my mind what I was going to say. 'I am from British television, Your Holiness. Could you please give us a special Easter message?' I made up my mind to speak slowly because I knew that the Pope did not speak perfect English and, as he got nearer and I got more nervous, I realized that neither did I.

Then, there he was, standing in front of me accompanied

by his retinue. He raised his eyebrows questioningly and I stuck out my hand. As he gently shook it, I blurted out 'I'm from British television.'

'Good luck,' said His Holiness with a smile, and moved on to the person next to me who had someone to introduce him. Bill Ward, never a man to admit defeat, motioned for me to get as close as possible to the man with whom the Pope was chatting and pretend that I was joining in the conversation. This I managed to do, nodding away in the direction of the Pope's back. Fortunately, it did not turn out to be too bad and, although we did not get our Easter message, we got away with it.

We had started filming in bright sunshine, with blue skies over the city producing sparkling pictures for the first couple of days. Then one morning we woke to find that there had been a snow storm in the night and Rome was under a foot or so of snow. The temperature had dropped and it was now bitterly cold. This made things difficult for me because I was only wearing a blazer and flannels and, as I had already conducted a couple of interviews dressed that way, for the sake of continuity I had to continue to wear them, shivering my way through the rest of the songs while cameraman Tom Ritchie had to shoot everything from underneath so that the snow didn't appear on the pictures.

One lunchtime when we were filming near St Peter's Square, we all piled into a little restaurant that had been recommended to us by Monsignor Bill Purdie, an Englishman who was then the Press Officer at the Vatican. He came with us to make sure we would get a good meal. Myra was there, and Ronnie Cass and his wife Valerie, along with Bill Ward and the rest of the crew. During the first course, Monsignor Bill and I were discussing opera and he started singing a snatch of the duet between Rudolfo and Mimi in the first act of *La Bohème*. I started humming along with him, and soon we were doing the whole duet between us.

'We can't both be Rudolfo,' he said. 'I'll have a go at Mimi's part.'

There were very few customers apart from ourselves, so I didn't feel too embarrassed. Then the proprietor came to our table and encouraged us to sing some more. Bill Purdie opted out and suggested that I should sing something on my own.

'If you sing "Cantari" for me,' said the owner, 'I will give you a bottle of a very special wine which I only keep for myself.'

'Go on,' said Myra. 'We can take it home with us.'

And so I sang it, slightly higher than I would normally have done, and Ronnie was beginning to worry about me bursting a blood vessel. However, I finished with a couple of ringing top notes and everyone applauded generously.

'Grazie, signor,' said the proprietor, producing the very special bottle of wine he had promised me. To Myra's chagrin, he proceeded to open it there and then and poured it out for everyone. As a non-drinker, I had to be satisfied with a Diet Coke, but I had a good laugh and so did Myra, who claimed the empty wine bottle. 'If we come back tomorrow can we have a refill?' she said, jokingly.

'Yes of course!' said the proprietor, his eyes lighting up. 'We can arrange a special price for you.'

'No thanks,' I said, looking at the remains of my Diet Coke.

We managed to get both programmes finished on time and when they went out there was not a trace of snow anywhere, but some viewers did wonder why my nose had gone blue halfway through the Easter *Highway*.

Our travels during the making of *Highway* took us to many places outside the British Isles. We did three programmes from the Holy Land, two from the Falklands, a Christmas special from Orlando, Florida, one from Malta, a Remembrance Sunday programme from Caen, one from

Majorca, in which I tried to show viewers my own view of the island that has been my second home for over thirty years, and one from Lapland, when we flew up to the Arctic Circle with a plane-load of underprivileged children for a visit to Father Christmas. Roy Castle came along on that trip and won the hearts of everyone on board.

He had worked out a little dance on skis, which he was going to perform in the snow. There was great consternation when we kept getting reports that there had not been a snowfall for quite a while. Then, the night before we were due to fly from Gatwick, we got the news that the flakes were coming down at last. Someone up there loved Roy.

The whole trip was organized by the staff at Gatwick Airport, who paid for the chartering of the plane and presents for the children – all of whom had a really wonderful time.

Incidentally, it was a *Highway* from Gatwick Airport itself that produced the highest ratings we ever had – eleven million viewers tuned in to watch that programme, on which Barry Sheen was the principal guest – although it says a lot about the show that our average viewing figure was eight million.

One of the things I enjoyed most about *Highway* was the recording of the music. There was always a great atmosphere in the studios at Wembley CTS and the musicians were nearly all old friends of mine – some from pit orchestras in the theatres I had played, some from Wally Stott's orchestra, who provided the background music for the *Goon Show*, others, like the great trombonist Don Lusher, from my days with Philips.

We usually fixed the band call to start at ten o'clock in the morning, which meant my leaving home at seven o'clock to get to the studio in time for a run-through with Ronnie and Ted Brennan, who was the conductor for all the *Highway* music sessions. After we had got all the banter out of the way, we would then decide the tempos of the songs I was to record and discuss the interpretation of them. Most of the material consisted of hymns I already knew – I reckon I have sung my way through *Hymns Ancient and Modern* with only a few exceptions, and I'm no stranger to the Methodist Hymn Book either. But there were also new songs to record and I welcomed the challenge they presented.

By ten o'clock the orchestra would be in place with their parts set on the stands by Ted who, with Ronnie, had arranged the music. I never ceased to be amazed at the ability of the session players to play the music at first sight. After going through the first piece a couple of times, the recording engineer Dick Lewzey would ask me to sing a few bars with the orchestra to get the right sound balance and then we would put down the track. Sometimes I would record up to eight songs in two sessions and, when you consider that each song had to be sung three or four times to get it right, it could be a bit of a strain.

Apart from the very popular hymns like 'The Old Rugged Cross', 'Abide With Me', 'How Great Thou Art' and 'Onward Christian Soldiers', the greatest number of requests came for a song, the lyric of which was sent in by a viewer and set to music by Ronnie Cass. The song was called 'Cover Me With Roses' and the lady stipulated that she was to remain anonymous and that any royalties her words earned were to go to the Musicians' Union Benevolent Fund to repay the pleasure musicians had brought into her life.

One of the pleasures that *Highway* brought to me was the privilege of singing with some of the greatest musical talents in the country. Sir Geraint Evans and I sang the big duet from *The Pearl Fishers* on his boat in the marina at Aberayron. Unfortunately for me, on the trip out to his boat I managed to get my trousers very wet. I bet that was the first time that duet had been sung with one of the singers having a wet bum.

In a *Highway* from Portmeirion, the fantastic brainchild

of William Clough Ellis, I sang the same duet with that brilliant young baritone Bryn Terfel – this time with dry trousers. Helen Field, the little Welsh soprano with a terrific voice, joined me in the first duet from *La Bohème* – the same one that I did with Monsignor Bill Purdie in that restaurant in Rome – in a programme from Merthyr. Delme Bryn-Jones and I sang another duet from that same opera, 'O Mimi Tu Più Non Torno' in the magnificent setting of Sherbourne Castle. Ian Wallace was once brave enough to join me in 'The Gendarme's Duet', and Cleo Laine and I sang a duet from her and John Dankworth's lovely home outside Milton Keynes.

Apart from the music on *Highway*, some of the readings became very popular with our viewers. One was 'Death Is Nothing At All', which was beautifully read by Bernard Cribbins on the 1985 Remembrance Day programme from the beaches of Normandy. The words were written by Canon Henry Scott Holland (1847–1918) and had been sent in by Mr L A Maxim of Sudbury, Suffolk, who told us that they had been read at his wife's funeral service. He hoped that they might bring comfort to others. Well, they certainly did. We had so many requests for the piece that eventually we had the text printed in the *TV Times*. I think it's well worth seeing it once again in print.

Death is nothing at all – I have only slipped away into the next room – I am I and you are you – whatever we were to each other, that we are still. Call me by my old familiar name, speak to me in the easy way which you always used. Put no difference into your tone, wear no forced air of solemnity or sorrow. Laugh as we always laughed at the little jokes we enjoyed together. Play, smile, think of me, pray for me.

Let my name be ever the household word that it always was. Let it be spoken without effect, without the ghost of a shadow on it. Life means all that it ever meant. It is the same as it ever was, there is absolutely unbroken continuity. What is this death but a negligible accident? Why should I be out of mind because I am out of sight? I am just waiting for you, for an interval, somewhere very near, just around the corner . . . All is well.

I was very sad when *Highway* was eventually taken off the air because it had become an oasis of calm on a Sunday evening, giving viewers a chance to reflect, to revisit, from the comfort of their armchairs, places they may have been to in the past, the opportunity to hear good music and perhaps find comfort and inspiration in the tales of fortitude in adversity and the selflessness of those who spend their lives helping others.

Apparently the reason given for closing down the programme was because it was not attracting the kind of audience that the commercials were being aimed at – a case of God versus Mammon. We had a tremendous amount of mail from viewers who were highly indignant that the show was no longer going to be the high-point of their Sunday evenings, and quite a number of letters were written to the newspapers expressing anger at the decision.

After *Highway*, I went on with another religious programme called *Sunday With Secombe*, a two-hour Sunday morning show that I co-hosted with Kay Adams. It was a Scottish Television production, directed by one of the nicest men I have ever known, John MacDonald, and lasted for thirteen very happy weeks. It went out live, which meant that we were provided with an autocue – a device that fits over the camera and brings up the words on a screen in front of the lens. It is worked by an operator who feeds the words through the screen at the speed of the presenter's voice. There's nothing to it, once you get used to it. Unless it breaks down. That's when the viewer at home becomes aware that the presenter is looking blankly into the camera with nothing to say, until galvanized into action by a command in his ear-piece from the director to get on with the next item in his script.

This happened to Kay and me in a show from Scotland. About ten seconds before we were due to go live, the autocue broke down and, when the red light on the camera came on, we were both smiling inanely with nothing to read. Fortunately, Kay grabbed a script from an assistant standing nearby and handed it to me. 'Ah yes,' I said, breathing a huge sigh of relief and tried to read it upside down until Kay turned it the right way up. A very resourceful girl, Miss Adams! Between us we carried on with the programme, alternately reading from our scripts, and nobody seemed to notice that there was anything wrong.

And now I have come full circle again. Last year I was asked by BBC television if I would like to present half a dozen *Songs of Praise* programmes. I was very flattered because, although we had been opposing each other during the life of *Highway*, we always had great respect for each other's work. After all, we said, we're working for the same Boss.

It was a standing joke when we were filming on location for *Highway*, that if a plane flew over or a lorry went past during a critical point in the action, the cry would go up, 'There goes the *Songs of Praise* plane', or 'Thora's driving that lorry'.

Although I have changed jerseys, so to speak, I am very happy to be associated with our old rival and comforted by the fact that I still have Ronnie Cass and the Ted Brennan boys playing on my side.

Pickwick Again

It was sometime in 1992, when *Highway* had finished and I was contemplating semi-retirement, that I received a phone call from Leslie Bricusse asking me if I was interested in doing *Pickwick* again. I had never really given it a thought, and said that perhaps it might be a retrogressive step – afterall, it was twenty-nine years after we had first opened at the Saville Theatre. 'I'll think about it, Leslie,' I said, and put the phone down.

Myra was not too keen on the idea at first. 'You're seventy-one now, and you're a diabetic, remember.' She was worried that my voice would not be able to stand the strain. I belted out a couple of verses of 'If I Ruled the World' in the kitchen, making all the cups on the table rattle and sending Vincent the cat running for cover. 'All right, you've made your point,' said Myra. 'Ask the kids what they think.'

Jennifer was all for it because she had grown up with the music, and so had Andrew, who also urged me to have a go. David, who only vaguely remembered the show from touring with us in America, was equally enthusiastic. Katy, who had not been born when it was done the first time and was slightly jealous because the other three had, threw her weight behind the decision that the old war-horse should have one more gallop into battle.

Jennifer said that since I had been doing *Highway* for ten years, a lot of people would have forgotten that I was an actor and comedian before I became a presenter of religious programmes.

I was secretly pleased at the offer, and asked Tony Boyd, who had taken over Jimmy Grafton's agency after Jimmy's death, to contact Leslie Bricusse and find out what his idea was. Since dear old Bob Kennedy had died too, I was missing his friendly advice, although I still maintained my office in St James's Place, manned now by my secretary Ruth Levine and Egon Painz, my business manager.

Ronnie Cass, whose opinion I have always valued, advised me to have a go, assuring me that, vocally at least, I would have no problems.

To cut a long story short, a meeting was arranged between Leslie, Tony Boyd and a couple of Leslie's associates and it was agreed in principle that I would star once again in *Pickwick the Musical*. There were several meetings after that, some at our house, where I met Patrick Garland, who was to be the producer. We had met once before when I interviewed him in Chichester for a *Highway* programme. He was the artistic director of the renowned Chichester Festival and, as 1993 was to be his last year in the job, the idea was to have *Pickwick the Musical* as his crowning achievement if I would agree to do it.

'In for a penny, in for a pound,' I thought. And, in truth, I knew I would be getting more pennies than pounds if I took the job, because everyone playing in the Festival had to settle for a salary far less than they would normally receive. But it was a challenge I was determined to take – after all, how many other actors had the opportunity to recreate a musical role thirty years after he had first performed it?

The deal was struck and it was now time to cast the show. After the débâcle on *The Four Musketeers*, I wanted to have some say in the casting, or at least have the chance to approve the choice of cast.

Patrick and I got on very well together and obviously, because of his well-deserved reputation in the theatre, I was prepared to accept his word on actors of whose work I had no knowledge. When he suggested Ruth Madoc for Mrs Bardell I was delighted because I have known Ruth since she had written to me as a young girl asking for advice about how to get into show business. I passed her letter on to Frank Barnard, my agent at the time, and he was a considerable help to her.

Glyn Houston, Donald's brother and a very fine actor, was my own choice for Tupman, but Patrick rightly thought that Glyn would make a great Buzfuz, doubling the part with that of Wardle, the brother of Rachel Wardle who runs off with Jingle, and the father of the two daughters for whom Snodgrass and Winkle fall hook, line and sinker.

The part I was most anxious to see played by someone with whom I could establish a rapport was that of Sam Weller, the boy who becomes Pickwick's valet. It was very important that he should be a person with whom I could get on, both on and off stage, because our relationship was essential to the success of the whole production.

'I know just the man for the role,' said Patrick. 'He's very versatile and he has a marvellous sense of comedy. His name is David Cardy.'

I took Patrick's word for it and crossed my fingers that when I met David the chemistry between us would work. I need not have worried, because he was the best possible man for the part. He has a great sense of comic timing, which is about the rarest thing to find outside the old variety performers and, as a bloke, he was very easy to get on with – the nearest choice to the great Roy Castle, who had played Sam

Weller on Broadway all those years ago.

The part of Sam Weller's father, Tony Weller, was a tricky one to cast at first, until Leslie and Patrick suggested that perhaps Roy Castle would play him. I was delighted at the thought that my old mate might be able to do it, but we all knew that he had been diagnosed as having lung cancer. In fact I was one of the first to know of his illness when he phoned me on the day his doctors told him. However, at that stage the news on his condition was more hopeful, and he had just successfully gone through his first bout of chemotherapy.

When he agreed to play the part of Tony Weller my joy was complete. The whole country was aware of his battle with cancer, and his appearance in *Pickwick* would give him a goal to focus on.

Michael Howe was a new name to me, but when Patrick told me that Gillian Lynne, who was going to be the choreographer, had highly recommended him for the part of Jingle, I accepted her choice with alacrity. I was feeling very happy about the prospect of working with Gillie again because, since she had been responsible for *Pickwick* in America, she had enjoyed fabulous successes with *Cats* and *Phantom of the Opera*, and travelled the world supervising and choreographing ballets and operas. We were going to be lucky to get her to stay still long enough to get the show into production.

The cast that finally assembled in Chichester for the first rehearsal was as good as the one that had been such a success thirty years before. There was one member of the chorus of whom I was particularly proud: Katy had been determined to work with me and had auditioned for the Bird Seller and as understudy to Ruth Madoc. She got the job – and a free lift down to Chichester with the star of the show.

Kevin Ranson, who played Tupman, also understudied my part and at our first musical run-through, I was relieved to find that he was more than capable of singing all my songs. Peter Land was a flamboyant Snodgrass and Robert Meadmore, a tall, handsome baritone, played against type as the timid Winkle. Everybody in the company could sing well, and the choral work was better than it had been the first time – and that's saying something.

Any doubts I had about my voice being able to cope with the demands of the show soon vanished after the first band call. I managed the top C in the number that closed the court scene with no bother at all and earned a round of applause from the cast who, if the truth were known, were also wondering whether I could make it.

The rehearsals were pretty gruelling, especially for the dancers, and Katy declared that she was aching in muscles she didn't even know she possessed. Gillian was a hard task master, but no one could complain because she never asked any dancer to do something that she herself could not. Even though she was well into her sixties, she could out-dance the lot of them – and there were some extremely good ballerinas in the company.

The stage at the Festival Theatre is of a modern design, being almost a theatre in the round, with the audience at very close proximity to the action because there is no orchestra pit. We all made our entrances and exits through the gangways used by the public to get to their seats, and quite often the odd latecomer was surprised to find Mr Pickwick himself lurking in the shadows as they climbed the stairs to the auditorium. There was no curtain and no overture; there was also a kind of show within a show which began about a quarter of an hour before the printed show time, when various members of the cast would wander around in the auditorium in full costume, chatting up the customers in lusty Dickensian fashion. Katy yelled herself hoarse trying to sell birdcages, and one of the girls who had apples in a basket actually sold them on the first night to the people in the front row – which caused some consternation with the property master who needed them for the first scene.

It was strange at first getting back into the Pickwick outfit, which bore a very close resemblance to the one I wore back in 1963. I had kept the original flat-topped hat that I had worn in the Broadway production and I clung to it as my lucky mascot. I had written the words of 'If I Ruled the World' on the inside of the lining, along with odd cues that I was anxious not to miss.

What I found somewhat terrifying on the first night was the fact that the only way I could see the conductor was on two small television screens mounted over the front gangways. Fortunately for me, the conductor, Ted Brennan, my faithful friend from *Highway* days, knew how nervous I was about missing my music cues even when his baton was practically up my nose, let alone fifteen feet away on a television screen, and he armed himself with a baton with a light at the end of it and all went well.

The advance bookings for *Pickwick* were quite phenomenal and everybody from the cast to the usherettes was hoping for a good first-night audience. I had heard that the Chichester lot could be sticky on the opening show, so there were plenty of 'Break a leg' and '*merde*' salutations among the cast, and a very special wish for success for dear Roy.

Myra, Jennifer and the grandchildren had filled my dressing-room with so many floral arrangements and pot plants that I thought I might catch greenfly. Incidentally, I shared my dressing-room with Prunella Scales, who was appearing in *The Matchmaker* on the nights we had off. We left many messages for each other, each vowing to see the other's performance, but unfortunately we never actually managed to do so.

I made my first entrance from the gangway in front of the stage, with my knees beating a tattoo as I walked and the lenses of my wire spectacles clouding over. David Cardy,

God bless him, whispered 'Good luck, guv'nor', and I got a round of applause before I even opened my mouth. My nervousness vanished, and I was back as 'Samuel Willoughby Pickwick' once again.

The set, by Poppy Mitchell, who had designed the *Plumber's Progress* set, was not as complicated as the original Sean Kenny one, but was very effective, with stage-hands dressed in black manoeuvring the trucks into their different positions to become the outside of Fleet Prison, then the inside, and then, in a burst of light, transforming into the George and Vulture at Christmas time.

Everything seemed to go well that night. We had done a couple of preview performances, but nothing can compare or be as important as the first night. The critics are out there, and nothing concentrates an actor's mind better than that fact. Although these days – unlike in the past – a critic can no longer be the cause of the closing of a production, their notices, if they are very bad, can have an effect on the box-office.

At the finale there was generous applause for all of us, Roy Castle getting an especially warm reception and, as we sang the reprise of 'If I Ruled the World', the company received a standing ovation, the first at the theatre for many years.

At the reception in the foyer after the show everyone was very complimentary. Patrick Garland gave me a big hug and thanked me for a great performance, as did Gillian Lynne. Cyril Ornadel, who had written the music for the original show, made the journey from his home in Israel to be there on the first night and Wolf Mankowitz, who also remembered the first opening night thirty years back almost to the day, gave me a thumbs-up sign. Like Roy, Wolf was undergoing chemotherapy and had made a special effort to attend the performance.

I slept well that night.

When the reviews came out, I was 'Tinkered', 'Spensered'

and 'de Jonged' in the *Daily Mail*, the *Sunday Times* and the *Evening Standard*, but the local press were ecstatic. There was a time when a bad notice would have sent me straight to bed with my head under the pillows, but those days have gone and I'm more philosophical. I remember the occasion during the North African campaign when, in the process of obeying a call of nature, a neat hole suddenly appeared in a cactus leaf above my head. My first instinct was to straighten up and shout 'Hey, watch it! You could kill somebody like that!', and then I realized that that was exactly what the enemy rifleman had in mind. I was a legitimate target – and so I am when I brave an audience. The only consolation is that firearms are forbidden in the theatre.

We had a wonderful season at Chichester and the idea was to play five weeks in a London theatre before going on to Birmingham's Alexandra Theatre for the Christmas season.

For reasons I'm not too sure about, the publicity for Sadlers Wells was late going out and we played to poor houses most of the time. It was a period that I called the Valley of the Shadow, because there is nothing more dispiriting than trying to squeeze laughter from a sparse audience. I was glad that Roy was not with us for those five weeks, because it would have been very hard work for him. At the end of the Chichester season he had begun to look very ill again and though he was contracted for Birmingham I had grave doubts about him being able to make it.

The company was very supportive during the time we were at Sadlers Wells and David Cardy and I began to think up ways that we could liven up our comedy scenes together. I'm afraid that I became rather outrageous again in the bedroom scene, but Ruth, like the good trouper she is, joined in with the ad libbing and we found laughs between us that Dickens had never intended.

Throughout the five weeks at the Wells, we were sustained by the news that the advance box-office in Birmingham had topped a million pounds. We couldn't wait to get there.

After we had finished in London, I took a couple of weeks off at our home in Majorca to prepare for the season at the Alex, and when I returned to the company we were all set for a successful time. Roy was back, looking better than he had in the last week at Chichester, and, naturally, everyone was glad to see him.

We opened to full houses and the production took on a new sparkle after the pessimism of the previous five-week season. Then, after the Wednesday matinée of the week before we were due to finish, with notice-boards outside the front of the theatre proudly announcing 'House full for second performance', we were all summoned back on to the stage to be told that the theatre had to close there and then. There was to be no evening performance and there was no money available to pay any of the cast.

It was a tremendous shock to everybody, and we all sat in the stalls afterwards while it was explained that the theatre was now in liquidation on the orders of the City Council. Even the theatre staff were being sacked. We were asked not to 'rock the boat' by commenting adversely to the media about the closure in case there was some last minute miracle that would save the situation. Most of the kids in the show were in tears, and poor Roy, who was being sustained by working in the production, looked absolutely shattered, worse than I had ever seen him. Ruth and I went on television later that afternoon to talk about the closure, choosing our words carefully because we did not want the public at large to think that *Pickwick* was coming off because business was bad.

Outside the theatre, the audience was starting to arrive for the evening performance and finding that the tickets they had bought in advance could not be honoured. People were milling around in the street complaining about the cancellation.

I do not know the exact reason for the closure, but there was talk that our advance booking money had been used to shore up other productions and, when the management went to the corporation for yet another grant, they were turned down.

It seemed that the rest of the tour that was planned for the show was now in jeopardy. We were supposed to return to Birmingham for a further two weeks after the end of the Christmas run, and then go on to Woking, Sheffield and Norwich. Obviously, the fortnight in Birmingham was now out of the question, but the managements of the other three venues had such good advance bookings that they formed a company between them, called P W Productions, and put the show on themselves.

Patrick Garland and Gillian Lynne were in the same boat as the rest of us as far as not receiving any money for the last two weeks at the Alex was concerned, and were prepared to go along with the new company. It was a gamble that paid off, and the two weeks in each theatre proved profitable for us all.

Sadly, Roy, who had been delighted when the tour had gone ahead and struggled on with his role, was to make his last appearance at Norwich. By this time, he was failing again – although his grin never wavered and no one could have guessed from his performance that there was anything wrong with him. But, backstage, in the dressing-room he shared with David Cardy, Roy had to lie flat on his back all the time he was off stage. At the finale of the show, I used to bring him forward for a special bow and every night without fail, the audience would rise to its feet and give him a standing ovation. There was such a tremendous wave of love and affection for him that those who were privileged to work alongside him were engulfed by it and the tears flowed freely from us all. He was a constant source of inspiration and he always had time for other people. Even in the last week at

Norwich, when the weather was very cold, he would stand outside the stage door with his woolly hat hiding his now bald head, signing autographs and chatting with his fans.

He made the decision, along with his wife Fiona and his family, to meet his cancer head-on and in full view of the public, so that others could benefit from his illness through the Roy Castle Cause for Hope Foundation and the International Centre for Lung Cancer Research, the first of its kind in the world.

Before he died, Roy rang me in Majorca to wish me goodbye. He knew that his fight was over, and he just wanted me to know that the drugs he was taking would soon make it impossible for him to talk coherently. I found it extremely difficult to speak, leaving unsaid all the things I really wanted to say.

'I've seen the other side,' he said, 'and it's beautiful. I'll see you there.'

Three days later, Fiona rang me to say that Roy had passed away, and suddenly the world was a sadder place. He epitomized everything that is decent and good in the profession he had enhanced with a boundless talent and the courage of a lion. I still miss him.

Pickwick is still alive and kicking, having toured for a couple of years with Christmas seasons in Bristol and Manchester. This year, we'll be in Oxford for Christmas and then – who knows? – perhaps it will be time to put the old fellow to bed. And yet, and yet . . .

Grande Finale

The trouble with writing an autobiography is that with such a broad canvas to fill, it is inevitable that a lot of people and events will be left out. Things one always meant to include but forgot . . .

. . . Like the time Myra was presented with a beautiful bouquet of flowers on our arrival at Bermuda airport, only to have to hand them back when it was realized that the flowers were meant for someone else . . .

. . . Like the time when, during a week's variety at Cleethorpes, a young comic had to use a caravan in the car park of the theatre as a dressing-room, and consequently had to trek through the mud to get to the stage door. I had the number one dressing-room all to myself, so I invited the lad to share it with me, and that was the first time that Bruce Forsyth had a star on his door . . .

. . . Like the time that Mario Lanza and myself were on the same Command Performance bill and he was miffed because I was singing opera in the first half of the show. His minders had to lock him in his room to stop him getting drunk, but we shook hands on the stairs of the Palladium foyer as we waited for the Queen to greet us . . .

. . . When Myra and the Crown Princess of Japan had a long chat at the Buckingham Palace reception before the wedding of Prince Charles and Lady Diana. In a room full of very tall people, they were the only two who could see eye to eye . . .

. . . When I had to make a speech at a Variety Club luncheon to honour Lord Louis Mountbatten, and I opened with 'My Lords, distinguished guests, fellow barkers and,' turning to his lordship, 'Hello sailor!' He laughed . . .

. . . When, after the first time I had ever performed for an hour alone on stage at the Blackpool Opera House, I had come off feeling ten feet tall and Bob Kennedy, my faithful manager, came towards me with his hand outstretched. 'Good old Bob,' I thought. 'He's overwhelmed.'

He came up to me and said, 'Give me the keys to the car, you're blocking the stage door.'

. . . When Tommy Cooper told me the story of when he was in the Welsh Guards, on duty one night outside Windsor Castle. He had dropped off to sleep standing up in front of his sentry box. Suddenly he became aware of a light shining in his face as the duty officer approached. With his head still bowed, Tommy said a loud 'Amen.' And straightened up to attention.

. . . When the manager of the Garrick Theatre in Southport, after making an unsuccessful attempt to remove me from the bill, actually growled at me like a dog whenever he passed me back stage.

. . . Like the day when Johnny Franz discovered he had vertigo. He was driving in the Alps at the time.

. . . When I was told the story of an actor playing the part of Baron Hardup in a pantomime up north who tragically died of a heart attack in his dressing-room in the middle of the first half. The manager went on stage in the interval to announce the fact that 'Baron Hardup is unfortunately dead.' Back came the reply, 'Oh no he isn't!' And he said, 'Oh yes he is!'

. . . Like the most hilarious luncheon I ever had. Billy Connolly and me finished directing traffic outside the restaurant.

. . . When Eric Sykes and I were on safari in the middle of Uganda amongst a very primitive tribe called the Karamojong, who wore nothing but a long strip of cotton with a hole in the middle through which they put their heads, Eric got out of his bed, without a stitch of clothing on, and said, 'Give me my spear, I'm going shopping.'

. . . When I did a concert at Pentonville Prison and finished by singing 'Bless This House', which had the prisoners in hysterics.

. . . When Lionel Bart came up to me at a reception at 10 Downing Street in Harold Wilson's time in residence and said, 'Your flies are undone.'

'Come off it, Lionel,' I said, not bothering to check and walking in to the next room, where I became involved in a conversation with the Governor of the Bank of England and two Cabinet ministers. I thought I had them enthralled as they listened open mouthed to my views on the European Monetary System, until a waiter whispered in my ear, 'Your flies are open, sir.' And they were.

. . . When, along with Dame Vera Lynn and Sir Cliff Richard, I was invited to lead the community singing outside Buckingham Palace as part of the 50th anniversary of VE Day celebrations. At the reception in the Palace after a truly moving and inspiring concert, the Queen came over to talk to me. Noticing that my bar of medals had come adrift, Her Majesty fixed them back in position. 'There,' she said, giving them a pat. Then she smiled – and at that moment I would have climbed Everest for her.

This is the time, I suppose, at nearly the end of what has been known in the family as THE BOOK, originally referred to with a kind of reverence and, as time dragged on, gradually recognized as 'the sword of Damocles over Dad's head', that I should sum up the seventy-five years that I have trodden this earth. The best way to do this is in the form of an obituary I have prepared for myself.

He was born in 1921 in Swansea, South Wales, to a Mr and Mrs Secombe, from whom he took his name. The first sign of Secombe the creative artist appeared when his parents acquired a gramophone. He took to leaping about the house to the music, wearing the boots the doctor had suggested as a support for his weak ankles. He also took to wearing lampshades and his mother's hats. His parents exchanged worried looks, and one day his father presented him with a pair of boxing gloves. He put them on his head.

His scholastic achievements were few. Overshadowed by a brilliant elder brother and a clever four-year-old sister, he turned instead to sport. He was caught carving his initials on his desk during a maths lesson, and was told by the master that he was for the high jump. He won the event easily and followed it up with a superb win in the three-legged race, from which he was subsequently disqualified when it was realized that he was running alone.

Perhaps the turning point in his life came when he joined the church choir. He revelled in the old hymns, forever trying to sing higher and louder than anyone else. In this he succeeded so well that his solos in the church concert were performed from behind locked doors in the vestry, in order to protect the stained glass windows.

He was forced to practise hymn singing alone on the hill behind his house and even then, with a following wind, his top notes played havoc with the glass houses on the allotment a mile away. This made him very unpopular with the neighbours.

World War Two arrived in time to save the situation. He was called up with the TA, to the delight of the rest of the council estate who formed the first ever Adolf Hitler fan club in wartime Britain.

His Army career was undistinguished until he was sent out to North Africa in 1942, an event which changed the whole course of the war.

'I was at a troop concert in Tunisia in December 1942,' said Major-General Sir Brian Cobblers from his home last night, 'when this little fat Lance Bombardier came on stage. He did some unfunny impressions and then he began to sing. My God, I've never heard anything like it. Windows shattered and men dived for cover as his top notes broke the glasses in the officers' mess. I sat there deafened by the noise and then, quite suddenly, it came to me: why not harness this terrible power, turn it against the enemy and get myself a KBE?

'That night, we drove Secombe out into the desert and placed him in a large round hole, immediately in front of an Italian division, with instructions to begin singing "O Sole Mio" at 4.30 am precisely.

'For two or three minutes there was no reaction at all from the other side. Then pandemonium broke out. White flags waved; men reeled about, clutching their heads and sobbing piteously. "Please-a stop," cried the Italian commander, brokenly. "We give-a in."

'My strategy had worked. Secombe the Sonic Songster Mark One was born, and, under conditions of great secrecy, we used him again and again throughout Europe. Believe me, if he had not developed laryngitis at Arnhem, we would have been in Berlin in 1944!'

After the end of the war, Secombe drifted into show business, managing to control his voice to a reasonable level, though at one performance at Blackpool Opera House, he managed to unleash a top C that opened the swing bridge at Warrington.

His subsequent appearances on television were always recorded in the presence of an ear surgeon and a glazier. The Rose Window at York Minster had to be boarded up when he sang there.

Success of a sort came his way – he acquired a wife, an agent and four children, though not necessarily in that order. He was written up in the popular papers and written down in the intellectual ones. He suffered fools gladly because he was one of them and, like all performers, he was basically insecure. This was to be expected from someone who once said of his career that it was built on such shaky foundations as a high-pitched giggle, a raspberry and a sprinkling of top Cs.

PS. We are now settled up on the hill, with Jennifer living close by with her three children, Harriet, Emily and Sam; Katy, at present a member of the National Theatre Company, has a house nearby; David is married to Judy, a brilliant young publisher, and they have a lovely little daughter called Florence; and Andrew is married to the actress Caroline Bliss and they will have had their first child by the time this comes out.

My cup runneth over.